Handling Conflict and Negotiation

INTRODUCING THE SERIES

Management Action Guides consists of a series of books written in an Open Learning style which are designed to be

■ user friendly

■ job related

Open Learning text is written in language which is easy to understand and avoids the use of jargon that is usually a feature of management studies. The text is interactive and is interspersed with Action point questions to encourage the reader to apply the ideas from the text to their own particular situation at work. Space has been left after each Action point question where responses can be written.

The Management Action Guides series will appeal to people who are already employed in a supervisory or managerial position and are looking to root their practical experience within more formal management studies.

Although Management Action Guides is a series of books that cover all aspects of management education, each book is designed to be free standing and does not assume that the reader has worked through any other book in the series.

Titles in The Management Action Guides series are

Making Effective Presentations

Managing People and Employee Relations

Achieving Goals Through Teamwork

Planning and Managing Change

Creating Customer Loyalty

Handling Conflict and Negotiation

Handling Conflict and Negotiation

MANCHESTER
O · P · E · N
LEARNING

KOGAN
PAGE

First published in 1992 as *Negotiating and Handling Conflict* by Manchester Open Learning, Lower Hardman Street, Manchester M3 3FP

This edition published in 1993 by Kogan Page Ltd

Kogan Page Limited
120 Pentonville Road
London N1 9JN

© Manchester Open Learning, 1992, 1993

British Library Cataloguing in Publication Data

A CIP record for this book is available from the British Library.

ISBN 0 7494 1140 6

Printed and bound in Great Britain by Biddles Ltd, Guildford and Kings Lynn

Contents

GENERAL INTRODUCTION

The message will come through time and again in this book that, in handling conflict and negotiation, your acquired skill - how you do something - is just as important as what you do and far more important than what you just know.

As a manager or supervisor, you need to be constantly mindful of the broad aims and objectives of your organisation as you perform your daily work. The responsibility for inculcating the organisation's 'values' in those you manage cannot be passed on to someone else. It is your job. You are in the front line.

This responsibility is not light, and the particular aspect of it dealt with in this book is especially demanding of your skill and resourcefulness because

■ it requires you to address situations in which emotion plays as much part as reason

■ as a result, it requires you to concentrate not only on your knowledge and experience but also on your personal qualities, eg. your patience, manners and even habits

■ if you do not shoulder the responsibility, small problems escalate and disruption results

If, in the midst of this, it would help you to have a focus to keep in mind the overall aims of your organisation; **then remember these simple, connected, propositions**

■ an organisation's main asset is its staff because only people, not machines or procedures, can achieve excellence

■ people would not be able to achieve excellence if they were not imbued with their own strongly held set of values and beliefs

Your responsibility is to harness those human qualities for the benefit of the whole, and only by knowing how to handle those occasions when those differing values and beliefs come into conflict, as they inevitably will at times, can you gain the benefit that only people can provide.

The **aims** of this book, therefore, are to

■ show how the skills of negotiating and handling conflict fit into the overall job of the line-manager

■ analyse what is meant by 'negotiating' and by 'conflict', showing how they may manifest themselves in the context of the job of a line-manager

■ stress the importance of a good staff relations background to the successful resolving of conflict

■ help you identify the many forms and causes of conflict

■ develop an overall approach and set of techniques for handling conflict and negotiating positively and purposefully

1 AN ENVIRONMENT FOR DOING BUSINESS

In order for a company to excel in the 'marketplace', it has to encourage openness and innovation in its employees. This encouragement is especially important for you as a manager or supervisor. It is your job to ensure the smooth running of your department with as few inter-personal and inter-departmental conflicts as possible.

In this chapter, then, we shall firstly examine the **concept of 'negotiation'; and the significance of negotiation in first creating, and subsequently maintaining a healthy organisational environment.**

Although it is inevitable that you will have to deal with conflict of some sort or other sooner or later, we shall see that the climate which you create and encourage will be a significant factor in how much conflict you may have to deal with. In particular, we shall examine the right of your staff to know what is expected of them. In return, they will want to know that they have a right to be heard whenever they need to express themselves. We shall also look at your staff's need to know the reasons behind any decisions you take that concern them. All of these points are conducive to a good climate in which your staff can excel and put their trust and respect in you as their line-manager.

ACTION POINT 1

Think of two instances, either inside or outside your working life, where you have been able to innovate or improve something with the help of an environment that encourages innovation and invention.

Then try to recall two instances where you felt stifled or discouraged from contributing your ideas or action.

Briefly describe these and explain how the encouragement or discouragement manifested itself.

Now continue with the text.

Wherever there are people there will be conflicting ideas, values, beliefs, styles and standards. Handling that conflict is an important skill in all walks of life. Moreover, it is vital in a business which founds its purpose on people rather than things.

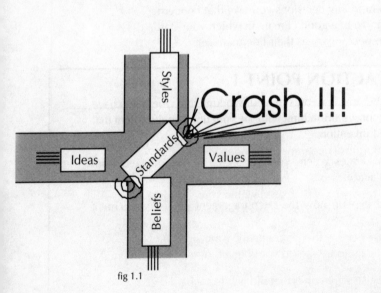

fig 1.1

This means that

- you must be more knowledgeable, skilful, patient and resolute than your predecessors

- your options in any given situation are much more numerous and varied than before

As management becomes more flexible, dynamic and personal, so must the handling of conflict. Action which might end a conflict but, at the same time, quashes an idea worth exploring, creates a distrustful atmosphere or dissuades the talented but less assertive people around you from contributing their skills, is not good enough. Nor is its opposite, the tolerance of conflict and the fostering of disagreements that make for a discordant, unproductive atmosphere.

ACTION POINT 2

Recall an occasion when you contributed something to your working environment which proved successful and for which you were congratulated in some way. Were there any side effects, good or bad, in terms of relations with your colleagues? Were any previous relationships altered in any way? Write down your comments in the space below and compare them with the suggestions that follow.

You may have noticed that your contribution changed your superiors' and peers' perceptions of your ability and potential. You may have started to communicate better with some new group or department and opened up easier channels of discussion.

Admiration, trust, respect and loyalty may have increased within your group. Alternatively there may have been some discord, jealousy or resentment.

The point is that it is impossible to succeed without altering the way you fit in with and are perceived by your colleagues - either to your benefit or loss.

One of the few things that psychologists agree on is that old habits are harder to break and to replace than new ones. In the same way, harmful or negative conflict is more easily handled by prevention at the earliest stage, and it is for this reason that you must be in the front line when it comes to handling conflict - not simply as a functional response to the pressures of 'productivity' or quantifiable targets, but as an opportunity to install the right attitudes and values where they might have been lacking. You must be able to recognise the elements of conflict, handle it quickly and positively, and channel the forces that gave rise to it away from discord and in the direction of the company's long-term objectives.

ACTION POINT 3

Think of a recent occasion when you dealt with an instance of conflict and could have used the opportunity to remind the participant(s) of why the conflict was harmful to the department/company. Given the opportunity again, what would you say or do to get that message across?

Your comments should illustrate that no context is too mundane or insignificant to be used as an opportunity to put across your shared objectives and beliefs.

1.1 NEGOTIATION IS DOING BUSINESS

As a line-manager who is concerned with the positive aspects of management - setting and meeting targets, improving performance, setting new goals etc - it could easily appear that the need to negotiate, for whatever reason, and to handle conflict between whichever individuals or groups, are somehow negative functions of your job. At best they can appear to be irritants or distractions from your overall purpose. It is easy to imagine that an ideal world would be one where, once objectives had been set, everyone got on with their tasks unquestioningly and unwaveringly, looking neither left nor right.

Not only is this clearly unrealistic, it is also far from ideal. **It is only because people question and look around them that any progress, business or otherwise, can be made.**

Consider the following examination of 'Negotiating'.

It may seem obvious that management will at some point involve negotiation. What perhaps is not obvious is that, in an important respect, management, essentially, **is** negotiation. The word conjures up images of bargaining, across-the-table talks, bartering, arguing, resolving, demanding, conceding. All of these can play some part, but it is useful to note where the word comes from. 'Negotiate' derives from a Latin word which simply means 'to do business' - that is to go about your work and pursue your interests. This will almost inevitably involve **interacting** with the work and interests of others.

It requires no agenda, no table, no minutes, no money, no positions. **It simply means two or more parties with interests to pursue find that, to pursue them, they need to come into contact with and address the interests of each other in the search for mutual gain.**

The substance of negotiation could concern anything and everything: as important as preserving world peace or as trivial as erecting a garden fence. It could involve the whole world or just two neighbours or colleagues. It could take a lifetime to achieve or be over within seconds.

It is all negotiating and it all concerns you, all of the time.

fig 1.2

ACTION POINT 4

Without going into any detail, think of ten different activities, from the world stage right down to your own workplace or domestic life, which are, in essence, negotiations.

As well as the obvious ones, try to think of some that are less obvious but which meet the criteria above.

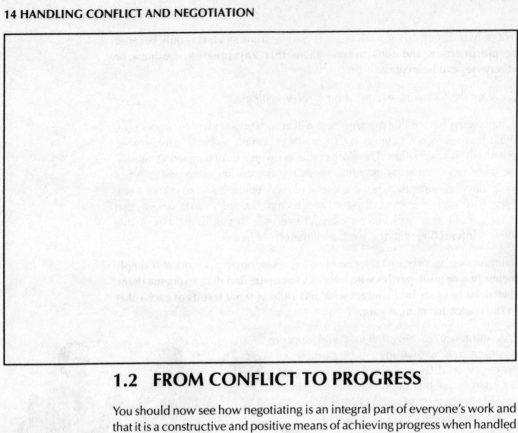

1.2   FROM CONFLICT TO PROGRESS

You should now see how negotiating is an integral part of everyone's work and that it is a constructive and positive means of achieving progress when handled properly.

But how does conflict fit into this outlook on work?

In their book 'In Search of Excellence' Peters and Waterman refer to homo sapiens as, 'the ultimate study in conflict and paradox'. They discuss at length the reasons why the 'rationalist' approach to management does not lead to excellence and conclude that its preoccupation with mechanisms, figures, orders, power struggles and quantifiable results requires people to be rational all the time - which, quite clearly, they are not. They are capable of rational thought and action but are also creatures of habit, stores of values and centres of belief. They are susceptible to emotional stimuli and capable of emotional response.

Peters and Waterman's findings show that the organisations which recognise those facts about people - both employees and 'customers' - and create a style of management that harbours and actively promotes these human characteristics are the ones that succeed in the marketplace.

At this point you should remind yourself of the title of this book. It refers to handling conflict, not suppressing it, banning it, tolerating it, or ignoring it. To use those approaches towards conflict requires minimal knowledge of its causes and its nature. But to handle it, and to handle it well, requires you to know all its attributes.

Why '**Conflict**'?

The contexts in which people conflict within a working community are almost infinite, but there are some basic reasons why people are prone to it.

The psychologist Ernest Becker identified a dualism in people's relations with their fellows: people need to be part of something and to stand alone, to conform and rebel, to be part of something greater than the sum of its parts and yet to be individuals who stand out from the rest. Peters and Waterman set this proposition in the working context and conclude that to get the full potential out of people in a collective, working situation, you have to provide them with the ability to assert themselves and to view themselves as individuals with control over their own destiny. In the words of Peters and Waterman, 'If there is one striking feature of the excellent organisations (they were referring to industrial/commercial organisations, essentially, but their observations relate equally to public organisations!) it is this ability to manage ambiguity and paradox'.

This is your responsibility - to manage 'the whole' (the uniting objectives and values of the organisation) by managing 'the parts' (the individualistic and independent people who work for it).

No matter how much people may agree on ultimate objectives, they will all have differing views on how to achieve them. They will also have differing beliefs, standards of behaviour, manners, priorities, personalities and senses of humour and show every facet of humanity that could possibly be evident in the working context. They can all lead to conflict and all need your awareness as a manager.

Why '**Progress**'?

Your task is made not only easier but also more purposeful by another basic human trait identified by Peters and Waterman. From this trait, conflict has the capacity to be transformed into progress if managed properly.

People do not simply differ, they also consider themselves generally as winners in certain fundamental ways. No amount of

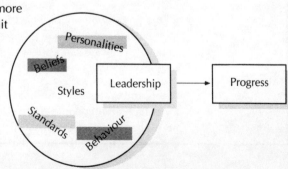

fig 1.3

rational proof that someone is just average in these contexts will stop people from feeling better than average.

The authors identify two contexts in particular

■ the ability to 'get on' with people
■ the ability to lead

To those one could add, from general observation of life

■ having a sense of humour
■ knowing and practising high standards of behaviour

You could probably think of more still.

As well as a whole host of individualistic beliefs and values, people are also blessed with a conviction that they can co-operate, influence, recognise and promote high standards and, when all else fails, look upon their situation with good humour - and do it all to a higher than average standard.

Your job is to encourage and foster those human traits in a way that will allow people's differences to be absorbed in the pursuit of the common goal.

ACTION POINT 5

Taking into account what you have just read, think of 5 examples of the way people exhibit their

(a)   conformity in the working context

(b)   individuality in the working context

Explain briefly if and how these tendencies clash with each other.

1.3 THE RIGHT CLIMATE

It is important to remember that the way you conduct your 'staff relations' will shape the attitudes that your people will bring to bear on future problems and difficulties and how strongly they feel committed to the department of which you are the leader.

In our present context, that means that the general climate you help create will to a large extent dictate how conflict manifests itself, how much or little damage it does, and how it is resolved.

Natural Justice

You have seen how encouraging a constructive climate - one that is open, supportive and tolerant - allows the different talents and resources of your team to be utilised.

At the same time your authority, credibility and capacity to influence your staff will be immeasurably strengthened if there is a palpable sense of natural justice in the working atmosphere. This concept originates from and is normally associated with the legal world, but much of what lawyers mean by the term equates with commonly held moral standards and with the principles of good employee relations. You should have no problem in adhering to these principles in the workplace.

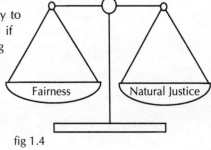

fig 1.4

The principles of 'Natural Justice' include

- the right to a hearing
- the presumption of innocence
- consistency and absence of bias
- the notion that laws should precede judgement
- the right to individual treatment
- the right to speak in your own defence
- the right to know the reasons for a decision

These principles are couched in legalistic terms but they are clearly the kind of values that would apply in any large organisation.

Their value is not just in their implementation but in their very existence - the fact that they are there if needed, that people can work in the knowledge that they can expect to be treated justly if anything goes wrong. Getting that feeling across is what you need to do from the outset of your managerial career. Without it, the trust, creativity, innovation and care that you are striving to attain will be that much harder to coax out of your people.

ACTION POINT 6

Some, but not all, of the principles of Natural Justice are, as we have seen, equally applicable to the working context.

Try to add to the list above 'natural' or 'commonly held' principles of justice or fairness that you believe have an important part to play in working relations.

Which of all the principles do you think is the most fundamental in a working context?

Write your ideas down, then continue with the text.

The principles of natural justice or fairness that are relevant to the workplace can be condensed into three fundamental precepts of good staff relations. They are the right to

- know what is expected of you
- be heard
- know the reasons for a decision

If your staff relations are conducted on these lines in all their many guises you will have created the right climate in which to deal with individual conflicts.

Let us now look at how you can create that climate of natural justice in the workplace.

1.4 THE RIGHT TO KNOW WHAT IS EXPECTED OF YOU

Be careful with this. It does not mean that someone in breach of a company 'rule' or informal code of conduct is blameless if they happened not to know that the rule or code existed. Just as in the legal setting ignorance of the law is no defence. In the business setting, it is just as much a person's duty to know what standards of behaviour are expected of them as it is the manager's responsibility to make them known.

What this principle means is that there should be clear and accessible standards of behaviour, particularly in the treatment of other colleagues, for all to follow - and that any conflict and negotiation procedures must only operate with reference to those standards. The rules must precede the process.

This principle relates, of course, to the techniques of good communications. In fact, the preventative value of establishing a good working and communications climate in your section can hardly be over-emphasised.

Letting the purpose of communication determine the form and delivery you adopt is a good way of proceeding. It is vital to select the right form of discussion for the particular purpose you have in mind.

Kinds of Discussion

Work discussions can be divided into four major categories according to their purposes. These are to

- give information
- get information
- work together to solve a problem
- reach an understanding or agreement

We might call them **announcement, discovery, problem solving** and **negotiation** respectively. How you conduct these different kinds of discussion will vary according to your purpose in holding the discussions.

Let's look at each in more detail.

Use this form when you want to give information to your people. In its simplest form, it consists of two steps

    (a)   giving the information

    (b)   making sure that information has been clearly understood by the other party

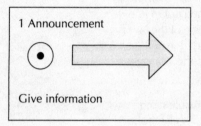

fig 1.5

When the information is short and simple, it is best to just give the information, then check for understanding. If the information is complex or involves many steps, it may be best to break it down into 'chunks' and give it to the other person one piece at a time.

Use discovery when you want to obtain information from another party. It is particularly useful in areas like fact finding, handling employee complaints etc. The two basic key steps are

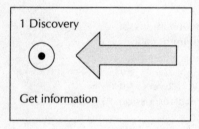

fig 1.6

(a)   getting information from the other party

(b)   making sure it is complete and accurate

This form of discussion allows you to get the facts - the relevant 'Who', 'What', 'When', 'Where', 'Why' and 'How' of a situation.

The third form of discussion is problem solving. It bears some resemblance to the two previous forms but it is different in several important ways. The most obvious difference is its focus on actions to be taken. The four key steps are

    (a)   give the need

    (b)   get a plan to solve the problem

    (c)   agree on progress checks

    (d)   summarise what part each is responsible for

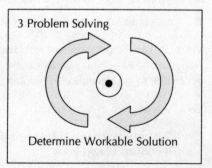

fig 1.7

These four items - need, plan, check, summarise - are the key steps involved in this form of discussion.

Use this fourth form of discussion when views differ. The purpose is to reach a mutual understanding or agreement. It requires that each party exchange some information; and to that extent, it resembles a combination of the announcement and discovery forms. But there is an additional element in negotiation. Once information is given and received, both parties work to reach mutual understanding or agreement. This entails three key steps

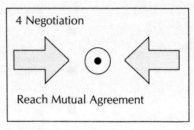

4 Negotiation

Reach Mutual Agreement

fig 1.8

(a)   giving

(b)   getting

(c)   confirming or clarifying

One of the more interesting aspects of the 'negotiation' discussion is that these steps are usually repeated more than once until clarity is assured. In fact, they may be repeated in the context of several stages or facets of the discussion (to reach agreement on the discussion process; to clarify positions and needs; to clarify the rationale or importance of positions etc).

You can lose trust by using a less direct and categorical form of delivery for something that needs a firm statement - just as you can endanger co-operation and cause resentment by treating an issue for negotiation as if it had already been settled and decided. **Points to remember** are

■   if there has been a clear breach of discipline say so

■   if you have some company policy to communicate then do so clearly and assertively

■   do not invite comment if comment is superfluous

■   do not give the impression that there is an alternative if you know that there is none

■   do not sound apologetic if you know that what has to be said will be unpopular - your management position will be instantly undermined

On the other hand if

- you need to gauge the feelings of your staff, do not assume that they know that their views are welcome. Tell them

- you are looking for a better way of implementing some policy then ask for suggestions

- your role is to start a negotiation - to make an offer - then make it explicit that is what you are doing

- you or management above you have no fixed view on a subject and are looking for suggestions, before you make any proposals start with a question, not a proposition

---

ACTION POINT 7

Using the four kinds of discussion described in the text, decide the correct form of delivery for each of the situations given below and write down your answers.

1   Scotching unfounded rumours about changes in working conditions.

2   Stopping some slight but unacceptable 'picking on' a new team member.

3   Resolving a long-standing grudge between team members.

4   Finding out why a previously happy and productive team has suddenly become less so.

5   Trying to accommodate everyone's feelings about smoking at work.

6   Asking that something done below standard be done again.

You may be interested in comparing your answers with ours which are as
follows

1   Announcement

2   Announcement

3   Negotiation

4   Discovery

5   Negotiation

6   Problem Solving

ACTION POINT 8

Examine the following sentences and write down which kind of discussion you
think has been used for each one. Then write down which methods of approach
should have been used in each case.

1   I'm sorry about this, but I've just got a directive from the manager and it says
that our loading procedure has to be changed because of product alterations
- again! What do you think?

2   We have got to sort out those tea breaks. We can't have everyone going at the
same time like yesterday. I've worked out this timetable. Here it is.

3   The Manager wants to know what we all think of the new inter-site travel
arrangements. Anyway, here's a copy of what I've sent.

4   I've been watching you two arguing all morning. It has got to stop, do you
understand? Your private battles are not for fighting here. Clear?

You may be interested in comparing your answers with the following

1   Was problem solving, should have been announcement.

2   Was announcement, should have been problem solving.

3   Was announcement, should have been discovery.

4   Was announcement, should have been negotiation.

Use Theme and Cue Techniques

You should employ the techniques of Theme - Outcome - Cue, as used in the following examples

Theme

Cue   (Announcement)

Theme

The tea break system appears not to be working.

Cue   (Negotiation)

I would like us to get together and work out a schedule we can all stick to.

Theme

I think it's clear to both of us that the new system isn't working well - we're always rushed at the end of the week.

Cue   (Problem Solving)

What do you think is the cause? Can we sort it out quickly?

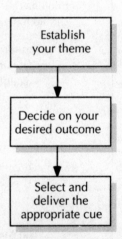

fig 1.9

Theme

I've noticed you've not been yourself today - you look disgruntled and uninterested in work.

Cue   (Discovery)

Is anything wrong?

Explain What Happens Next

Everyone is more co-operative and relaxed if they know where they stand and they know what is expected of them.

Vague, mis-cued, confused, deficient, apologetic or rambling communication is wide open to misinterpretation, both genuine and contrived.

How many times have you come away from a meeting, presentation, negotiation or discussion with your head crammed with information but with a nagging, growing feeling that you do not know what happens next. 'Am I to implement it?', 'Is it policy or just a suggestion?', 'Do they want me to do it?', 'Do they want it now?', 'Are they looking for comments?', 'Is there more talking to be done or can we get right down to it?' or even, 'Why do I have to know all that, what's it got to do with me?', 'Do they mean me?!'

ACTION POINT 9

Think of a meeting, announcement, discussion or negotiation you have conducted at work recently. Try to recall if you used the Theme-Outcome-Cue method. Do you think you made it clear to everyone what had to happen next? Note down your thoughts and ideas on how you might have done things better.

Ending a discussion with a purpose is clearly not something that comes naturally to everyone.

A **negotiation** should end with an **agreement** (even if it is only to continue talking) that is explicit, clear and unambiguous.

A **problem-solving** exercise should end with a **solution** and an action plan: what is to be done, by whom, where and when.

An **announcement** should ideally end with a **question** that simply asks everyone if they understand. Make sure they really do.

There are many reasons why someone will say they understand when they do not - lack of interest or motivation, lack of knowledge, lack of will to carry out orders, embarrassment at being the only one who admits to not understanding, and many more.

A discovery should end with your summary of what you think has been said and the questions 'Is that how it is? Have I missed anything?'

The potential for harmful conflict between people working in a flexible value-led management system is immeasurably reduced if you as a line-manager can apply the methods you have just read and let people know what is expected of them. **The resolution of negative conflict in such a system is made far easier where an atmosphere is created in which people know where they stand.**

1.5   THE RIGHT TO BE HEARD

Everyone has a right to be heard.

If people know that they will be heard whenever there is conflict, then at once you have eliminated the more negative effects of defensiveness, suspicion and resentment.

There are two elements to this

■ people with grievances or those involved in conflict or disciplinary matters, however informally dealt with, must have a hearing

■ hearing must be a right not a privilege

A Right not a Privilege

To ensure that everyone in your department knows that they will, not just might, get a hearing, you need to show in your everyday working behaviour that you value what they have to say, listen to their problems, and hear what they tell you.

Do not listen when you are distracted - if you are under pressure, set a time when you can listen and stick to it. If your work pattern makes some times easier than others to take time to listen, then tell your people at the outset so that they will know that their non-urgent problems will be dealt with.

Try to be a 'fly on the wall' - listen and gauge the feelings that your team has about you. Do they say to each other that they 'know where they stand' with you or that if you say you will do something you can be relied upon to do it? If they do, or say similar things, you are on the right track. If, conversely, they say that you sometimes speak or act just to deflect a problem or 'for a quiet life' you will need to take stock not only of your approach to managing conflict but also to your skills of time organisation, priority setting and stress-avoidance.

ACTION POINT 10

Why do you think it is important that a right is never treated as if it were a privilege or a favour?

Has this ever occurred in your working life? Have you ever been guilty of this? Explain the circumstances briefly. What would your reaction be if someone were only listening to you 'for a quiet life'?

Write your thoughts below then continue.

A Hearing Not Just a 'Listening'

You must not just listen to what your people say to you - you must also hear (which you will not do if you are distracted, no matter how hard you listen) and you must show that you hear, because if you

- listen without hearing your credibility will soon disappear
- hear but do not make it clearly, even exaggeratedly apparent that you hear you will be wasting an excellent opportunity to instil values into your staff

To go away from a hearing and put your jointly arrived-at conclusions into practice without the other party knowing that you are doing so is sacrificing open, flexible management for the sake of a narrow, 'efficient' outcome.

Remember you are dealing with emotions as well as facts, and in emotional circumstances there is an old adage that 'it's the thought that counts'.

> Listen, hear, say what you will do and do what you say.

It is important to remember that what is known as 'active' listening requires

- a calm, undistracted atmosphere
- eye contact with the speaker
- responsive facial expression
- appropriate body postures
- encouragement to keep talking
- paraphrasing, summarising, probing
- appropriate acknowledgement of feelings

to be effective. Remember the LISTEN mnemonic

- **L**ook interested
- **I**nquire with questions
- **S**tay on track
- **T**est understanding
- **E**valuate the message
- **N**eutralise your own feelings

Be aware that a hearing, however informal it may be, is a cathartic experience: it allows people to 'get things off their chest'. Inevitably something will have been brewing for at least a while - no matter how open your department's communication channels are, people will still let matters reach a certain point before they share their problems in the hope that the area of conflict will 'blow over'. By the time they reach you there will be at least some 'steam' to be let off. This cathartic role is vital but it is also a danger. To let people go away from your hearing with that feeling of relief so familiar to us all when tension has been defused and then not to act as you said you would, no matter what that action was, is certain to lower your credibility and to sour the atmosphere long after the event.

Do not allow your people to feel let down.

If, for whatever reason, you cannot deal with the problem, either because it is out of your competence, needs to be referred up, requires further hearings or because you simply do not know what to do and need to think or to ask for advice, then say so. Do not let a problem become a resentment

■   **listen** to what is said

■   **hear** what you listen to

■   **show** that you hear

■   **say** what you will do

■   **do** what you say

1.6   THE RIGHT TO KNOW REASONS

One sure way of alienating people is to give decisions concerning their behaviour or attitude, or to announce action that affects their working life, without giving adequate and clear reasons. The more contentious the issue, the more alienation results - to alienate all of your staff is unacceptable, to alienate half of it is a recipe for civil war.

People are alienated by the giving of decisions without reasons, or adequate reasons, because it is treating them as immature, unthinking and unimportant.

Giving carefully worded and relevant reasons for your decisions - even if those reasons are not accepted by everyone - demonstrates that a system of justice is at work and that you care that your people should feel as if they 'belong'.

To maintain that feeling of 'belonging' while, as sometimes you must, finding in favour of one person or group and against another, you must give reasons for a decision that are

- relevant
- clear
- consistent with each other
- objective
- based on fact
- re-usable in the same circumstances

and are not

- irrelevant
- vague
- contradictory
- personal
- based on assumption or rumour
- 'one-offs' or special treatment

Some examples include

'I want you to look at ways in which you can improve your attitude towards your colleagues because . . .

1	. . . we are all under special scrutiny at present and I don't want our department to get a poor reputation.'

2	. . . I know what your kind are like - given half a chance. You are born trouble-makers.'

3	. . . I have heard things I don't like the sound of. I won't go into detail - you know what I'm talking about.'

and

'I am moving you to another area of work, as of the beginning of next month...

4	. . . I know you are keen to develop your I.T. skills but I cannot afford your learning at the expense of the smooth running of the department.'

5   . . . I don't normally do this after such a short time but I just think in your case you're not going to make it in that sphere of work. The sooner we find your best 'niche' the better.'

6   . . . I just think you'll be better suited there. Anyway, things may change and we might be able to put you back where you were after a while.'

ACTION POINT 11

Look at the examples above. How would you describe the reasons given for the two decisions? Use the checklist above as a reference. Briefly describe why you would assign one of those descriptions to each example.

You may be interested in comparing your answers with the following text.

1   The reason given is irrelevant. A good attitude towards colleagues is important at all times, not just when the department is under special scrutiny. It could also leave the impression that good working relations in normal circumstances are not important. It does not ask for the pursuit of shared values but merely seeks an expedient solution to a temporary problem.

2   This is personalised and prejudiced. The person to whom it is addressed is immediately alienated. Their attitude has already been judged. They might as well line up to their reputation.

3   This is based on rumour. It may be true, half true, a version of the truth, false, or even a deliberate 'smear'. It is also vague. The person concerned does not even know what to do to present their side of the case.

4   This is contradictory. One statement gives a reason for moving, the other for staying. If the manager knows how eager the person is to improve, why do they not facilitate it rather than suppress it? Recognising a positive attitude in people while at the same time suppressing its expression in work for the sake of 'efficiency' is not an approach that should be tolerated in any work environment.

5   This is not a reason at all. It is a justification for 'one-off' treatment diagnosed not by reason or discussion, but by 'gut reaction' or a hunch. It is the product of a lazy mind and if it doesn't result in a feeling of victimisation it will certainly cast the recipient as a failure and so alienate them from the department or even the company as a whole.

6   This is vague and negative. The recipient has no idea what action to take in order to make progress or how long it might take.

ACTION POINT 12

Using the examples we have just looked at, rewrite each statement using two or three reasons for each case that illustrate the criteria of relevance, clarity, consistency, objectivity, being based on fact and being based on some generalised principle rather than arbitrariness.

You will hopefully have written something along the lines of the following

'I want you to look at ways in which you can improve your attitude towards your colleagues because'

(i)   we have all discussed the deterioration in the atmosphere and it became clear that your concentration on getting things done perfectly was having a side effect of discouraging the rest of the team from doing anything that might attract your criticism. I think a little more give and take would improve things without letting standards slip. (relevant)

(ii)   the particular examples we have looked at are types of behaviour that we cannot expect from someone in your position. (objective)

(iii)   although there has been a lot said that you have rightly shown to be exaggeration and gossip, those two instances of your conduct that we have talked about are not acceptable. (based on fact)

'I am moving you to another part of the department where you will come into contact with the public less . . . '

(iv)   because I think we both agree that your strengths lie elsewhere and you recognised that your character would probably not suit that kind of position in the long run. (consistent)

(v)   the normal trial period is now over and after a thorough appraisal we do not think an extension would tell us anything we do not already know. It was worth a try but I think we both see the merits of going back to your normal job. (based on precedent - not arbitrary)

(vi)   I am sure that a period of 3 months or so will give you time to judge what you prefer and will give me time to make my mind up whether we would like to have another trial period. (clear)

CHAPTER SUMMARY

Having completed this chapter you should now

- understand why your handling of conflict and negotiation needs to be positive and aimed at excellence

- be aware of the special circumstances of management in your organisation that require particular expertise from you in the sphere of conflict

- be able to practise the principles of good staff relations in order to create a climate which minimises harmful conflict and maximises your chances of resolving it when it does arise

If you are unsure about any of these areas, go back and re-read the relevant part(s) of the text.

2 CONFLICT: ITS TYPES AND CAUSES

To suppress or ban conflict requires minimal knowledge of its symptoms, forms and causes; to tolerate or ignore it requires even less. But, if you are to **handle** it, particularly in an organisation where people are highly skilled, highly motivated and treated in a flexible, adult way, you will need to know as much as possible about it.

You will need, therefore, to employ the skills of observation and deduction - and to do so professionally and objectively in times of stress. In particular, you will need to identify **people in conflict**, which will also involve the need to be able to **notice the existence of any conflict** which arises. In order for you to solve such difficulties which may arise, you will need to be able to get to the root of the problem by **discovering the causes of conflict**. You will also need to be sure that the **symptoms actually point to the cause** of any conflict among your staff. We shall examine all of these points in this chapter.

2.1   WHO CONFLICTS WITH WHOM?

The short answer to this is probably 'everyone, some of the time'. Conflict is so much part of human life that it would be difficult to imagine anyone who had never been involved in some kind of conflict at work.

Conflict is always between people, either singly or in groups of one kind or another. All kinds of things **cause** conflict - habits, ideologies, personalities, competition for resources and many more. We will be looking at these in detail later in this chapter.

However, for now, you should be aware simply of **who** can conflict with **whom**.

ACTION POINT 1

Think back over your last working week and try to recall examples of conflict which you were involved in or which you observed.

Look at the categories below and tick the box next to any which describe those conflicts. Then continue reading the text.

You or one or more members of your department in conflict with

1   another member of your staff

2   a group (formal or informal) within your department

3   your department as a whole

4   another line-manager on your level

5   your immediate manager

6   another superior

7   a member of someone else's department

8   a group (formal or informal) in someone else's department

9   someone else's department as a whole

10   the company as a whole ('the system')

The chances are that you will have ticked a good number of boxes but that those conflicts were small, did not disrupt your work or the work of whoever was involved and were generally 'all part of life'.

However, some of them may have been more serious and damaging to morale and a co-operative working environment.

If you have not ticked any boxes at all, try to remember the last time your own line-manager asked you to do something straight away when you wanted to get on with something else - or when another department demonstrated a set of work priorities vastly different from your own perception of the relative importance of the organisation's activities. Then go back and look at the list again.

The fact is we all conflict with each other for a good proportion of our time at work even if most of the time it is in some minor way. Most of the time, too, we are extremely adept at resolving conflict and, as a result, we hardly notice its existence. How many times have you been driving or been a passenger in a car on a busy road with parked cars on either side. A car comes towards you. There is only room for one to pass safely. In a moment, either because one is nearer the obstruction than the other is, or because one is going uphill and one downhill, or one of you is feeling generous and the other less so, there is a flash of headlights, a raised palm and you both pass by without upsetting each other or causing any disruption to the traffic around you. Nine times out of ten that is....

The point is that it will help you greatly while completing the remainder of this book to take a **broad view** of the concept of conflict and not to associate it constantly, in the working environment, with the cliché of management/worker disputes; or within the confines of an ongoing conflict which you may presently be involved in at work. Anybody can conflict with anybody else - **and it is just as important to be aware of those conflicts we regularly settle in a moment as those that become serious**. We can learn the lesson from the former and apply it in the latter cases.

fig 2.1

Whether conflicts are individual or between interactive groups (or even between large sections within an organisation that rarely come into contact but are aware, perhaps falsely aware, of each other's beliefs, behaviours and values,) those conflicts are quickly surrounded by, even encrusted in **emotion** and **feeling**. The more individual the conflict - the more eyeball to eyeball it is - the more emotionally will it be expressed. But even the most 'abstract' of conflict is susceptible to this human characteristic. Just as Phil may be furious at Caroline, so two departments can be incensed by each other.

In brief - conflict, at whatever level, is between **people** in all cases, and is expressed in **human terms** at every stage. Attempts at analysing or resolving it which do not take these facts into consideration are doomed to failure.

ACTION POINT 2

Using the categories in ACTION POINT 1, try to identify and explain the types of conflict illustrated by the following examples. There may be more than one variation in each. Do not attempt to identify causes at present - simply look for all the people or groups you imagine would come into conflict and very briefly explain why they might do so.

a)   The Vehicle Body Workshop and Vehicle Servicing Workshop both rely to a large extent on the same tools and materials. The head of each Section has been in charge for many years and has a small, loyal, closely knit team.

The head of the VB Workshop believes strongly in the importance of her section to the whole organisation - 'After all', she would say, 'this is what we are in business **for.'** (**It** does bring in a disproportionately large amount of income for its size!) The head of the VS believes his Section is the 'cinderella' of the organisation and that his staff are treated, individually or as a group, accordingly. Both Sections have to press their individual claims for resources in terms of people and materials.

In reality they are both adequately served but matters are clouded by differing perceptions. Things are further complicated by the fact that the VB Section Head has been closely associated for many years with the Head Of Department in charge of both Sections - they 'came up through the ranks together'. It is this Head Of Department who, on a day to day basis, allocates resources between the two Workshops. She notices a certain resentment in the VS Workshop and, to counteract it, treats the latter with special care when it comes to apportioning a particularly sought after resource (a new workshop) that both Sections covet.

(b)   Three secretaries - Margaret, Steve and Sue have worked together for 2 years looking after the needs of the Head of Department and Deputy Head. They get on very well and are extremely good at their job.

Margaret is 40, Steve 26 and Sue 19.

Margaret works for the Head and is also in charge of secretarial operations in general in the General Office. Steve works for the Deputy Head who may take over from the Head in 6 months time on her retirement. Sue is the junior and works for both Margaret and Steve.

They all know that the Head is about to retire and that the Deputy Head may well take over as Head. They also know that, when this happens, the Deputy Head post will not be filled, for the time being at least. (An existing line manager will act as stand-in.) There will then only be room for two secretaries. Steve will move up with the new Head, Sue will look after the Acting Deputy Head needs and Margaret will be moved sideways - to look after another Head of Department down the corridor in a department that constantly comes into contact with the Deputy Head's office.

One day, the Deputy Head comes into the secretaries' office at lunchtime to find Sue in tears. The old atmosphere has changed, she says, and she now spends most of her time acting as peacemaker between the other two. They are constantly getting at each other. She thinks that explains why work has been deteriorating.

c)   'It all started when Harry Jackson retired. She had been here donkey's years, knew the place inside out. If you ask me, he should have been the Manager - he would have done a better job. Anyway the fact is he knew us and trusted us. He treated us like adults. He knew we would get the job done - and done well - even if we didn't do it exactly to the book. There was a bit of give and take. And we never got any complaints.

Then this guy Moore turns up - tells us things are going to be different. He wants more 'systems' and won't let anyone take it easy - even though he knows we'll get the work done in our own way. Half the time he doesn't know what he's talking about with all his so called 'theories.'

'Have you talked to him? I mean personally, man to man. Tried to explain things. He will respect you - he knows the place runs because of you.'

'Well you can't. He keeps himself to himself. Doesn't want to know! If it's play it by the book he wants, he can have it. No favours from now on. Next time there's an emergency, he might just find we all want to go home on time.'

In (a) there is a classic group conflict based on perceptions of how they and 'the others' compare in the eyes of the establishment. There will also be a clash between the two Workshop Section Heads and probably between individuals from each team. The VS Workshop head will have a long term suspicion of the impartiality of the Head of Department which probably will not be removed by the short term palliative he is offered. Meanwhile the VB Workshop Section Head will conflict with the Head of Department, her old colleague, also, for treating her unfairly on this occasion.

In (b) it is likely that **everyone** will conflict with everyone else and there are the seeds of an inter-group conflict as Margaret moves to her new job and tries to re-establish her position **via that department** vis à vis the newly promoted, and younger Steve. Their respective bosses may well be dragged into dispute by virtue of their 'loyalty' to their respective secretaries. The poor junior will probably end up being the butt of everyone's frustration.

This is a time of flux. Everyone is trying to establish new positions. The old days when everyone's role was well defined and secure have temporarily gone. Such periods of flux are prime contexts for conflict.

(c) This is a case of a team, and each member of it, against an individual. They are all unhappy with change and with the new man's style. He is unsure of his position and wishes to assert his authority. Both sides have made up their minds about each other without communicating properly.

2.2 THE SIGNS OF CONFLICT

We have seen from the above examples that conflict can be expressed in many ways. Your awareness of conflict will involve you using your intuition as well as your rational knowledge. How often have you said that you can 'feel' that there is conflict, that things are not right, that you could 'cut the atmosphere with a knife'? Sometimes, of course, the signs of conflict are quite explicit - a furious argument, an exchange of angry memos, even a fight. But most of the time you will not be able immediately to 'put your finger on it' - yet you know that something is wrong - a cold look, an unreturned greeting, excessive politeness, work that is grudgingly done, lack of co-operation and so on. Your instinct will tell you so much but, as you have already seen, sometimes it will let you down or at least will benefit from some well practised skills.

fig 2.2

The fact is that, however much we would like to think it, none of us can sit in judgement like Solomon, impartially, objectively and wisely assessing situations and apportioning the outcome. Everyone is susceptible to emotion **whether or not** they are the ones involved in conflict.

The effect of this typically human character trait, in the context of **observing** and **identifying** conflict, can be summed up in one sentence:

> If you go looking for something, you will surely find it

If you approach a conflict situation with the attitude that can be expressed in sayings such as

■ 'I've seen this kind of thing before'

■ 'I know what they're up to'

■ 'I know their kind'

you will only observe those facts or tendencies that confirm your original diagnosis.

Just as if you have ever proof-read anything which you are **sure** is word-perfect, you will hardly ever see even the most glaring errors, so in conflict situations you will see only the symptoms that you are looking for if you have already decided on the cause.

Instead you must

■ approach conflicts with an open mind

■ accept that you too have feelings which may cloud or influence your judgement

■ look for **signs** first and **then** try to assess the cause

---

ACTION POINT 3

Think back to any conflicts you have observed recently.

How reliable was your instant diagnosis? Now that the conflict is resolved, can you think of symptoms which at the time you had not noticed?

Write your ideas down overleaf then continue.

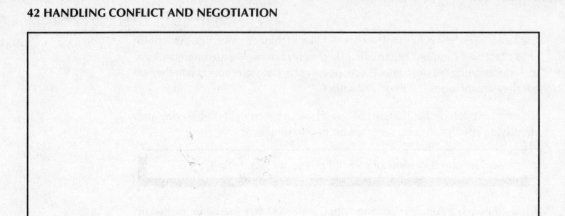

Professor Charles Handy, in his book 'Understanding Organisations' divides the signs of conflict into two types

1   Symptoms

2   Tactics

You may find this sub-grouping helpful in your observation and identification of the signs of conflict.

The only real difference between the two, however, is that **symptoms** are either unconscious or at least unintended instances of behaviour associated with conflict whereas **tactics** are the deliberate ways in which people involved in conflict express their position, 'make life difficult' for the other side and, in some cases, attempt to 'win' the battle.

Let us examine each in more detail.

The Symptoms of Conflict

The symptoms of conflict are as varied as their individual causes and as the people or groups that display them.

They can be

■   obvious - a row or fight

■   subtle - an atmosphere that is too quiet

■   active - a telling off or aggressive letter

■   passive - a 'sending to Coventry'

Some of the more common symptoms include

- deterioration in standards of work

- arguments

- avoidance of social contact

- tension 'in the air'

- a 'them' and 'us' vocabulary

- too much politeness or formality

- clock-watching

- lack of morale

The important point to grasp at this stage, however, is that **not all** of these phenomena are **necessarily** symptoms of conflict at all.

Lack of morale, for example, could be caused by a poor managerial approach to group or individual motivation, just as much as a feeling of antagonism towards 'them'. Arguments could result entirely from personal problems, in which case counselling might be the answer.

Be aware that many problems, some totally unrelated to conflict, produce identical emotions in people.

ACTION POINT 4

Think back over the last few weeks and see if you can add to the above list of **symptoms** of conflict any that were noticeable in your area of work.

Could any of them have been the result of causes **unrelated** to conflict? If so, what might equally have been the cause?

Write your answers and then continue with the text.

Your own **management style** will be evident in your handling of conflict as in all the rest of your tasks - you may by nature be an interventionist and take an active interest in the lives of your people or you may be one who prefers to stand back and let people get on with their own work and social lives.

Whatever the case, **you cannot afford not to get involved** when you see symptoms that **could** indicate the existence of conflict. In fact you should develop a style which is **curious** of people's behaviour. You should make it your business to be actively on the look out for signs of trouble - **not** with a view to making something out of nothing but with the aim of quickly establishing that either

■ the cause is **not** conflict but a private matter or a question of managerial style or

■ the cause **is** conflict and needs urgent attention or

■ the symptoms were illusory, you were mistaken, there **is no** problem and you can all get back to work with peace of mind

Turning a blind eye, for whatever reason, will neither solve the problem nor give you the peace of mind you need to get on with your job.

It should now be apparent that the symptoms of conflict are

■ extremely varied

■ not always obvious

■ sometimes identical to the symptoms of other problems

In order that you may more easily check out a possible symptom of conflict, you may find the following categories, suggested by Professor Handy, useful

Poor communications: People and groups of people either cease to communicate at all or do so perfunctorily and with an air of tension.

Inter-group hostility: One department, section etc is chronically at odds with another.

Inter-personal friction: Roughly from quiet tetchiness to open aggression.

Escalation: The problem is 'sent upstairs' not so much for settlement as for **backing**. Each side wants the manager, supervisor or whoever to end the conflict by **backing** the one against the other.

Proliferation of red tape: More and more 'bureaucracy' is created in order to stop someone or some group from doing things their way or even from doing anything at all.

Low morale: The feeling that 'it's no use trying' or 'why bother?'

ACTION POINT 5

Take the 6 categories suggested above and think of three examples of each that might occur in any working environment. If you think of one that does not fit into any of the groups or deserves a category to itself then add that to your list of six.

Write your answers and then continue with the text.

Remember too that in these examples, and doubtless in yours, there are some which could be caused by problems that have nothing to do with conflict - and some even that are not caused by problems at all. The people who clam up when you come into the room may just be organising your birthday party!

Be inquisitive but be open-minded

Tactics for Victory

If symptoms are unconscious, or at least unintentional or un-premeditated signs of conflict, then what Professor Handy calls 'tactics' are certainly conscious, intentional and probably pre-meditated.

That is the **only** difference, but it can be an important one when deciding on your **approach** to a conflict.

As an illustration of this consider the following examples

1   Alison and Barry have had a row over who was responsible for some electrical equipment safety checks being mishandled. They both have strong views and both have responsible attitudes towards safety. They argue, shout at each other, reach an impasse and retire to their corners finding it best to ignore each other's presence until one or other decides to give in and apologise. They don't speak.

Roger and Paula also have a similar row. Again they both have strong views and both have responsible attitudes to safety. They argue and reach the same impasse. Eventually Roger decides to break the ice. He thinks that safety should come first rather than the 'face' of either of the two colleagues, and that perhaps they should both seek the advice (and mediation) of the Head of Department. He suggests this to Paula. Paula doesn't want to know. She is determined to **win** the argument as much, if not more than, to have safety checks done her way. She does not respond to Roger's attempts at reconciliation. She wants to 'freeze' him out. Roger, rebuffed, feels worse than ever and sulks deeper into his corner.

2   Christine is a secretary. She believes she is being under-resourced to the extent that she cannot do her job properly.

Her supervisor, Malcolm, disagrees. He believes that, with more regard to efficiency, she could do the job satisfactorily without any more resources. Christine explains, asks, then pleads, but gets nowhere. She feels she is not getting the backing she deserves and 'cannot work with' the supervisor. She loses motivation. Efficiency suffers noticeably. Eventually she goes over the head of Malcolm and talks directly to the Manager, Bryan. When Bryan talks to Malcolm he becomes furious and feels betrayed.

Martin is another secretary who also believes he is being under-resourced. His supervisor, Joyce, disagrees. They go through the same processes as Christine and Malcolm. Martin then decides that, 'if that's how she wants it she will have to live with inferior work'. He will **prove** his point by making no real effort to do the best with the resources he has. He also thinks he could do Joyce's job better than she can, anyway. To make sure the unsatisfactory work is noticed by the Manager, and to make sure it is Joyce who takes the blame, he goes directly to the latter.

In both cases the resultant actions - the things you can **see** - are almost identical. The causes and eventual ends are also quite similar.

However here are two important differences in each pair

■   in each case, in the second examples the signs of conflict are deliberately manufactured **whether or not they would have come about naturally**

■   there is, in the second examples, an objective **in addition to** the functional one of dealing with safety or gaining more resources. It is to win the battle

Each case is one where a conflict needs to be identified and settled, but the second examples, the ones where deliberate tactics are employed, perhaps require disciplinary action as well as mediation.

There could well be small power struggles involving deliberate, if small, acts of sabotage going on in these examples. It is important that you try to establish where deliberate disruption is being caused and where it is not. Do not assume reductions in efficiency or breakdowns in communication are deliberate tactics or just unavoidable but destructive symptoms - **find out for sure**.

We shall be looking at ways of doing this later in this book. For the moment you should simply be aware that your analysis will significantly affect **how you conduct** your search for causes and your assessment of the treatment required.

Compare the following list of 'tactics', identified by Professor Handy, with groups of 'symptoms' you looked at earlier. You will see in each case a significant overlap or 'grey area' between the two sets of behaviour.

The Control of Information

Keeping people in the dark, letting them know only what you want them to know, letting people believe what is not true. This could be as important as one department depriving another of information vital to its operations or as trivial as one colleague not passing on a message to another in order to cause that person embarrassment.

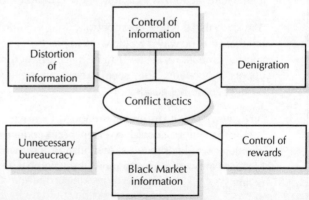

fig 2.3

The Distortion of Information

Telling one department one thing and another the opposite, playing one team member off against another, issuing different 'versions' of the facts.

Unnecessary Bureaucracy

Tying people up in red tape to leave yourself free to act.

Information Channels

Gaining and using the co-operation of people in key positions who can by-pass official channels. This can be as complex as setting up a whole 'black market' information system or as simple as having a 'friend' in the General Office who tips you off.

Control of Rewards

Deliberate sabotaging of someone's promotion prospects when they pose a threat or in retaliation for their actions.

Denigration

Tale-telling on a personal or group level. The 'tale' is told ostensibly as a piece of information relevant to the maintenance of good working practices, but is designed merely to denigrate.

ACTION POINT 6

Which of the 6 tactics above are involved in the following situation? Can you also identify any actions which are clearly symptoms rather than deliberate tactics?

'We knew that this new cost control system wouldn't work. It was all right on paper but there was no way it would work in practice. For one thing it is inflexible and for another it means we are tied to a PC half the day crunching numbers for those 'totter-uppers' in accounts. They seem to think we are here to move pennies around, not product consumer goods.

Anyway, we gave it a try and, sure enough, there were more things the system **couldn't** handle than things it could. We spent hours coming up with figures on paper that the computer wouldn't give us. And after all, they were only going to be read by the Management - and everyone knows they take no notice of them anyway. What a waste of time!

The trouble is that the new system really **was** wasting our time and I was going to make sure the boss himself really understood this. It was no use talking to Williams (the supervisor). He's very much on the make and this costing system is flavour of the month isn't it - so he wasn't going to back us up was he? So instead I just sent along exactly what the PC printed out - warts and all, with a nice long memo explaining that to fill in the gaps (and there were a lot of them!), would require my seeking permission for the direct data input people to do overtime - and we all know how taboo the word 'overtime' is these days! I did it when Williams was away on that conference and sent a copy to McGregor (the Head of Department) for good measure. Williams has got to start taking notice of what we **do** around here and stop crawling to that lot upstairs. When he came back and was called up to talk about the figures, I just gave him a copy of the print-out without a copy of the memo. That's all he asked for - that's all he got.

You should have seen the state he was in afterwards!'

2.3 THE CAUSES OF CONFLICT

It now remains to look at causes - to relate them to symptoms and to stress the importance of observing the latter but treating the former.

This is not as easy as it might appear. Using a medical analogy - for hundreds of years physicians, lacking the knowledge and technology of our day, continually treated symptoms not causes and often exacerbated the illness as a result.

Let's first look closely at some of the main causes of conflict at work.

If you study any example of conflict you have been involved in, it will quickly become apparent that, in an important sense, the **cause** has been the other person or group. Equally, that other person or group would see you or your group as the cause. Clearly, if it were not for 'another side', there would be no conflict. However, the existence of another party, although essential, is not sufficient. There needs to be some 'bone of contention' or at least some problem that creates the conflict between the participants.

There must be

■ an antagonist, willing or unwilling, against whom and possibly from whom conflict is expressed

■ an issue that binds two opposing forces in conflict

It is important that you bear these two elements in mind and that the connection between the two can be **direct** or **indirect**. You may, for example, come into conflict with someone over an issue that lies **between** you (a promotion you both want, or different views on how to do something, or even whether a window should be open or shut) and yet you can equally come into conflict with someone as a result of antagonism from another source (being criticised by your boss and taking it out on one or more of your own staff).

Bearing this in mind, let us look at some of the fundamental causes of conflict, with examples.

Professor Handy identifies two underlying issues

■ objectives and ideology

■ territory

to which you should add a third

■ 'irrational' hostilities

2.4 OBJECTIVES AND IDEOLOGIES

Any organisation with a discernible sense of purpose does not require or assume that every one of its constituent members has identical sets of beliefs, aims, philosophies and values. Such a perfect match between a 'corporate' entity and its parts would be undesirable even if it were possible. An organisation thrives on variety, the cross-pollination of ideas and the rigours of internal debate - it is likely to be a microcosm of society as a whole in the variety of points of view and character types that it employs.

So, whenever two or more people or groups whose aims and beliefs differ interact, there is always likely to be conflict of one kind or another.

Let us look at what is meant by objectives and ideologies.

Objectives

These could include such aims as

- to diversify into new areas of work
- to develop new methods of curriculum delivery
- to keep a 'tidy desk'
- to innovate
- to improve individual and group performance in the short term
- to improve in the long term
- to give due attention to Safety matters
- to keep expenditure to a minimum/cut costs

Even when all staff share the belief in the organisation's aims, are adequately and equally motivated and have trust in one another's integrity, their individual objectives, the roles they are expected to play or which they set for themselves, will continually diverge to some extent. Even when these 'sub-goals' are shared by a group of people, they will inevitably put differing levels of emphasis on one or another.

For example, one person's safety consciousness is another's obsessiveness, or one person's cost consciousness is another's missed 'marketing' opportunity.

So, even when you reach the state of motivating your staff and inculcating in them the overall aims of the company they will still differ in the objectives they need to set themselves in order to achieve those aims collectively.

ACTION POINT 7

Think of your own and other departments' immediate objectives.

Try to think of as many conflicting pairs of objectives as you can to add to the above list.

Write your answers overleaf and then continue with the text.

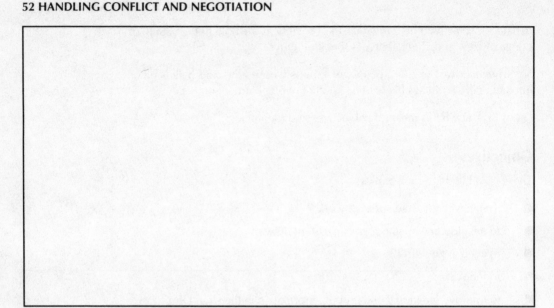

Ideologies

These are the value systems constructed consciously or unconsciously to accompany, unite and justify a set of related objectives. They are the bond of feelings, habits, manners, slogans and sayings of people who share objectives. Every group of complementary objectives will be a sub-set of an ideology. This is true of any type of large organisation. Let us take the case of a large commercial organisation to illustrate this point. Here, the Ideology-Objectives relationship might be set out as follows

Ideology	Objectives
They are in business to **sell**	To maximise sales To open new markets To be aware of customer needs
A good business is a prudent business	To cut waste To seek justification before spending To look at the 'bottom line'
Survival for them means diversification	Never being satisfied with existing service To want to spend more on X and Y To look at how others compare with your own standards

No matter how well you and your fellow line-managers spread the message throughout your organisation that a **common aim** should unite everyone whatever their job function, you are bound to come across these departmental ideologies and 'badges of office'. Indeed, to some extent they are each quite laudable and positive statements of economic fact.

However, they can cloud and obscure the overall mission if they are allowed to indulge in too much introverted self-justification. You will be familiar with the syndrome - it happens in all organisations to a greater or lesser extent. In the best organisations, it is open and light-hearted but in the worst it becomes vindictive and debilitating.

The important thing to remember is that, while conflicting **objectives** can be dealt with comparatively rationally and functionally, once they have become encrusted in an **ideology,** the process becomes that much more difficult.

ACTION POINT 8

Does your department or section have an 'ideology' or a metaphorical 'badge of office'? Do you have a rival or conflicting department or section? How would you describe your own group's ideology and how do you view the other group? How serious or light-hearted is the clash of ideologies? Is it ever harmful? Write your comments down then continue reading the text.

When Objectives Diverge

When objectives and their accompanying ideologies diverge, conflict will result which needs to be handled in a way that will encourage common objectives and broad organisational objectives to supplant the divergent ones. Again, an example from the world of industry is useful to illustrate this point.

Divergence and conflict

Lack of trust

Poor communication

Personal objectives

Poor listening

Deterioration and further conflict

fig 2.5

A production department in a Computer Hardware Company will be primarily concerned with meeting targets on schedule and within budget, while a sales department will be concerned with expanding sales and responding to customer demand. The result at a time of expanding activities could be a pressure on the production department to increase unbudgeted overtime, diversify in short uneconomic quantities and generally change schedules 'mid-stream'. One group may perceive the other as obstructive and rigid while that other may perceive the first group as wasteful and irresponsible.

This is where good communication skills, the creation of a climate of trust and the 'right to know what is expected of you' come into play. Where they are lacking or deficient, conflict will result and will build up the ideologies that separate the two groups so that next time the conflict will be worse.

To prevent or minimise these conflicts, the cause must be removed or, better still, not allowed to take shape at all. To achieve this management must

- create the right climate of trust
- communicate clearly and correctly
- re-emphasise the need to concentrate on common objectives
- listen, hear and respond to problems

As a manager, your staff will look to you as their leader to guide them, not only in what they do, but also in how they feel about their job. By all means enter into the light-hearted creation of an esprit de corps in your group, but never be tempted to let that prejudice your ability to focus your team's attention on common objectives.

Lead by example

Where Objectives are Unclear or Contradictory

Just as two people or groups with diverging objectives can come into conflict, so can a person or group come into conflict with his employing organisation as a whole (or any part of it) **when that person or group's objectives are unclear or contradictory**.

People need to know not only **what** they are expected to do but also **why** and **for whom** they are expected to do it. Where they do not, they will be subject to conflict, at first within themselves and later with their 'competing' bosses and 'the system' as a whole. This again is the fault of poor communication. People can sometimes receive two mutually exclusive requests in the same minute or two top priorities when only one is possible. In the longer term, conflict will be endemic if a person is put into a dual role where objectives and feelings of loyalty are split. In an organisation where hierarchies are not rigid, the need for communicating the **why**? and the **for whom**? are as important as the **what**? and the **by when**?

ACTION POINT 9

Try to recall a conflict you have observed or were involved in involving departments, sections, units or other groups where differing ideologies and objectives were present.

Summarise the respective ideologies in one sentence

■   what were the respective objectives?

■   what were the most visible symptoms of the conflict?

Have you ever been in a position where you were working towards conflicting objectives? Did this result in any conflict between yourself and either of the two people or groups you were working for? Did those two people or groups conflict over the issue of what you should be doing and to whom you should be reporting?

Write your answers below and continue reading the text.

Your answers to this ACTION POINT will be personal, but it is important for you to recognise the existence of such conflicts and how they arose in order to be able to avoid them more easily in future.

2.5 TERRITORY

We are all familiar with the concept of territorial establishment and protection in the animal world. Experiments that show what happens when territory is involved or overcrowding is imposed are vividly familiar. People too are fastidious establishers and protectors of territory and are equally irritable and aggressive when overcrowded. However, it does not end there. The 'territory' we are about to look at is not limited to physical space but to all other **finite resources over which people compete**. Those include

- space
- investment
- staff
- priorities
- equipment
- esteem
- influence
- power
- 'perks'
- financial reward

fig 2.6

All of these are the subject of competition and occasionally of conflict because of their highly prized and finite nature. There is only so much space; the training budget will only go so far; you can only do one thing first and so on.

The existence of these territorial boundaries which are occasionally breached is not always accidental or merely an undesirable side effect of working in a large organisation. Some, such as the limits of space in an office or workplace are just facts of life. Everyone would like more space available - including those whose unenviable job it is to allocate it. Some territorial battle grounds, however, are the result of deliberate and well thought-out policy. As resources such as investment, equipment and staff increase, there is a point where you start to get diminishing marginal return and even, at a later stage, a counter-productive effect. **More money** will only help to a certain extent and eventually an increasing amount will be wasted. **More people** will only add to efficiency up to a certain point where frustration, lack of motivation and low morale will creep in as **too many** people have too little to do and to take responsibility for.

Competition for territory is a cause of conflict because

■ some assets are naturally finite, and one person's gain is another person's loss

■ some assets are only assets when they are deliberately kept finite

In both cases, managers must see to it that competition is fair and calculated to lead to the general good.

The existence of territory can be signposted in a great variety of ways

■ a committee excludes as well as includes people

■ a set of 'unwritten rules' will define how far a group can run itself without outside control

■ status symbols and privileges will let observers know how senior their possessors are

■ published management decisions and policies will prescribe what resources are allocated to which departments

Although varied, these territories have a common feature: people are very protective of their own and mindful of the consequences of 'invading' someone else's. You will rarely invade someone's territory accidentally a second time.

ACTION POINT 10

Try to list 6 different examples of 'territory' prevalent in your area of work. Which of these do you prize the most and why?

Write your answers down then complete the following questionnaire. Try to answer each question as honestly as possible.

How would you rate yourself in terms of the following territories? Number each one on a scale of 1 to 5 where 1 represents **Very Protective** and 5 represents **Indifference** towards invasion of your territory.

Your work space

Your staff

Your privileges

Your salary ranking

Your status

Your title

Your tools or equipment

Your influence

The value of this exercise lies in the fact that by being aware of your own 'territorial' pride, you will be able to understand it in others more easily.

When Territory is Invaded

Conflict results when territory, in whatever form, is invaded either **accidentally** or **deliberately**, because two territories genuinely overlap or maybe the ownership of a piece of territory is disputed. These are not intended to be hard and fast categories and there are bound to be many examples that are in a 'grey area'. However, they may help you to analyse underlying causes.

Accidental

A new staff member innocently uses another person's familiar workstation.

A new staff member carries out a function that the 'older hands' have informally and traditionally viewed as someone else's.

Deliberate

An ambitious staff member carries out a task that normally requires their manager's prior approval.

A staff member wanting to impress colleagues uses too informal a greeting to the Managing Director.

Overlap

Two people who share a telephone both need to use it urgently at the same time.

Disputed

A Safety Officer and a Workshop Technician argue over responsibility for the implementation of safety checks in a workplace. They both have grounds for believing it is their job. Management has not made it clear in this case where policy ends and detail begins.

ACTION POINT 11

Identify the territories that are at the heart of the following conflict. How has the territory been invaded in this case? Which of the general categories above fits the best in this case?

An ambitious salesman takes aside a new colleague in his department and issues a 'warning' about lateness - not a friendly word of advice but something purporting to be 'official'. This is the job of a Head of Department and, in fact, this particular Head of Department was aware of the lateness and was about to 'have words' with the individual concerned, personally.

When Territory is Coveted

Sometimes there can be territories that do **not** overlap and are in fact well apart from one another. They share no common borders, and to invade one would mean trampling over several other territories in between - and yet the occupant of one, though never actually tempted to invade the other, will nevertheless look longingly at it from afar.

Some examples might be

■ the people who would love to know what their manager discusses in meetings and will not believe it when they are told, truthfully, that most of the time, nothing of any interest or moment takes place

■ the individual who longs for the freedom and responsibility that apparently come with management status

■ the manager who longs for the security and esprit de corps that comes from working in a closely knit team of specialists

The more distant the territory, the more unobtainable the prize, the more highly it is prized - and the more likely that resentment will result. It is a question of motivation and of needs. **If people cannot get what they want, they will want more of what they can get**, and the most obvious symptom of this will be the excessive protection of their territory (perks, status or whatever) that they are in charge of.

Luckily, most people do not let jealousy get the better of them, but a certain amount of tact and subtlety of observation **and** of treatment is required when you are dealing in an area where people's ambition, self-image or sheer curiosity are aroused but, for very sound reasons, cannot be satisfied.

ACTION POINT 12

Try to identify an example from your own working context where a tactful approach by yourself or other management is required in a situation of jealousy or resentment.

Briefly explain the situation and how you would approach it.

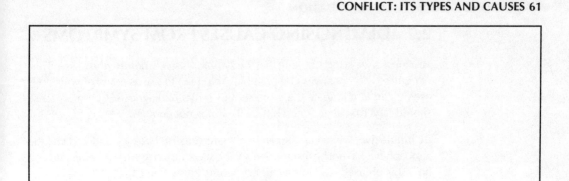

2.6 'IRRATIONAL' HOSTILITIES

Be careful with the word 'irrational'. Except in certain psychological disorders, hostility is always the result of a cause even if the cause is not one you could personally imagine resulting in hostility. However, hostility can be and often is totally unconnected in a causal sense with any objectives, ideologies or territorial dispute. The fact is that people sometimes just dislike each other. In social life they would never mix, perhaps even deliberately avoid meeting, almost inhabit different worlds. But in the working environment the oddest of couples are sometimes thrown together by the exigencies of the organisation's needs.

This kind of hostility can be the result of prejudices, private opinions or unconscious 'bad vibes'.

It is important to be very careful here. While it is entirely right not to force people who simply 'do not get on' to work together, hostility on grounds of race, colour, religion, sex or disability is totally unacceptable and, in certain circumstances, unlawful.

Another case of 'irrational' hostility is where someone is made angry or vengeful by the actions of their manager and takes it out on a subordinate or colleagues as a whole. These cases are perhaps the most difficult to deal with because the cause, even when it has been identified, is often impossible to remove.

This type of conflict requires a firm but understanding management approach. Warring factions often cannot, and sometimes must not, be separated. Counselling together with firm discipline is the only answer.

Cases of 'picking on' subordinates for something unconnected with them should be stamped out quickly as they are unfair and disruptive to morale.

2.7 DIAGNOSING CAUSES FROM SYMPTOMS

You must always try to be sure that the symptoms really point to the cause. This, of course, will not always be possible. You need to use as many of your skills as you can to eliminate the more serious errors of diagnosis. Common sense should never be abandoned but by itself it is not enough.

Be inquisitive, whatever your style of management. Look around and feel the atmosphere. Do not be distant. See and be seen. Listen to what is being said and how it is phrased. Get involved. Let people know you care.

Have an open mind. If you look for a cause that you have decided is there, you will find it. Do not prejudge the issue.

Look for symptoms. See if any might be deliberate tactics.

Talk to people. Use the level of formality or informality you think will get to the root of the problem. Use your communication skills. Select the form of discussion that suits the context, the person and the mood.

Listen and hear. Use your active listening techniques. Prime and probe to get the whole story. Summarise, paraphrase and ask for confirmation.

Confer and seek advice. Look at precedents, talk to others who look at the conflict from a different angle.

Do not make promises you cannot fulfil. Say only what you **know** you can do. Explain what happens next. Create a climate of trust that will help you get the whole story out in the open.

Do not take sides. There are usually two sides to a conflict. The more **obviously** impartial you are, the more you are likely to hear the truth.

CHAPTER SUMMARY

Having completed this chapter, you should now

■ realise the importance of understanding the nature of conflict at work

■ be aware of the great variety of people and groups who can come into conflict with each other

■ recognise the main symptoms and tactics of conflict in organisations

■ understand the importance of observation and be able to practise its skills

■ be aware of the main causes of conflict

■ see the importance of using all your acquired communication skills in diagnosing causes from symptoms

If you are unsure about any of these areas, go back and re-read the appropriate part(s) of the text.

3 SKILLS FOR HANDLING CONFLICT

Being able to recognise the existence of conflict is only part of the problem. You also have to know how serious the conflict is and be able to handle it properly. In this chapter, therefore, we will be looking at those skills you will need when handling conflict between two or more parties, where you are, in a sense, the mediator or resolver. In particular, we shall examine the need to understand **the relationship between healthy differences and harmful or negative conflict**. This will involve the need to develop the interpretive skills that will tell you **when you should and should not intervene**. It is, obviously, best to avoid conflict as much as possible, so we shall also be looking at the **skills that will minimise the risk of healthy differences turning into harmful conflict**. Inevitably there will be times when this is not possible, so we shall examine in this chapter the need to develop strategies and techniques for **resolving conflict professionally and positively**. In order to resolve conflict, you will need to develop good personal habits, so we shall also be looking at the importance of **being as objective and calm as possible in stressful circumstances** and separating people from problems, personalities from issues.

3.1 WHEN A DIFFERENCE IS NOT A CONFLICT

Promoting a working climate in which healthy, productive differences can legitimately co-exist and be expressed is essential for two reasons

- it allows innovation to flourish and improvements to be suggested and put into action

- it defines issues, tests solutions and imposes the rigours of debate on matters of common concern

The **fact** that differences are openly expressed sets the tone for the pursuit of excellent performance. The **act** of expressing those differences sharpens vague ideas into proven and tested solutions - or quickly consigns them to the wastepaper basket.

This latter phenomenon should be apparent in any personal context. How often have you harboured strong feelings or disquiet about an issue but been unable to 'put your finger on it' **until** you articulate your feelings in debate or argument and have to marshal your facts and back up your opinions with hard data. At that point the vague becomes concrete, the irrational is seen for what it is and discarded, and a nagging feeling becomes a well organised set of arguments. So it is in work. The expression of differences can illuminate problems, indicate solutions, refine arguments and defuse potentially harmful conflict.

Thus, a breakdown of co-operation which manifests itself clearly and without delay may suggest to you as a line-manager, that there may be an underlying structural or procedural fault that needs to be investigated and put right. Perhaps someone's job is being made impossible by a task allocated to someone else. Perhaps two people or groups have been asked, by different managers, to do substantially the same thing. An open atmosphere will prevent the cause from lying hidden and the problem from escalating.

Listening to options which members of a group had been sure did not exist can stimulate people to arrive at better solutions through the pooling of information. A 'face to face' dispenses with the need for third party involvement. Both sides hear the other's views at first hand. The effects of 'stirrers', rumour mongers and those who take pleasure in trouble-making are avoided. Being forced to put your views into words in an arena of debate quickly highlights the ones that are ill-defined, inconsistent, unsupportable or just plain nonsense.

Maintaining open discussion can lead to greater mutual respect between opposing people or groups. The ability to disagree with someone's views but be prepared to accept and even defend their right to hold those views can only lead to mutual gain. As Winston Churchill once said, 'Jaw-jaw is better than war-war'. The existence of a climate in which differences are openly and constructively expressed will stimulate those who are not naturally inclined to push their ideas to be more assertive and to contribute ideas that might otherwise have gone undiscovered.

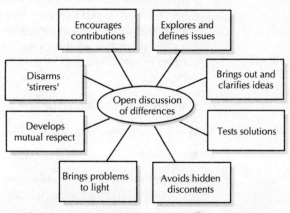

fig 3.1

ACTION POINT 1

Think back over the last few weeks and try to recall two or three instances of constructively expressed differences of opinion or belief. What benefits, if any, derived from these episodes? Were the differences resolved completely or merely clarified?

Your role in these situations is largely observational. To use a sporting analogy - the best rugby referees are the ones you notice the least, as a spectator or player. They see their role as facilitating the flow of play by applying the basic rules of the game and being flexible with everything else. They know that a certain amount of testing or 'softening up' will go on, particularly at the start of the game **no matter what they do**, and they only 'get involved' when conflict is **either** threatening one of the parties more than the other or where it is spoiling the game.

Similarly, your aim should be to

■ insist that established departmental/company procedures be followed

■ observe the expression of differences carefully

■ get involved when either one party or the stated objectives of the organisation are about to suffer

One tactic some referees use is to get involved early in a game to 'stamp their authority' on it, **whether or not** a real threat to a player or to the game exists. The value of this tactic is highly questionable and is

■   unfair (one side, arbitrarily chosen, has to suffer a penalty)

■   illogical and confusing

because it sets the standard of behaviour at an unreal and indeterminable level.

Your authority will be that much more secure and credible if you **always** intervene when, but **only** when, a real threat to one party or the shared objectives of your department or section occurs.

ACTION POINT 2

In which of the following conflicts would you get involved and which would you simply monitor carefully?

1   Two members of your department have a heated exchange on the way to the car park at the end of the day. You overhear snatches of their exchange and conclude that it is about their differing views on how to implement a new scheme of work.

2   Two members of your staff independently come to you complaining that the other is impossible to work with.

3   A number of your staff have fallen out among themselves. The atmosphere is cold and they seem to be forming into two factions. They talk to each other less and less as the days go on.

4   Two people who are known as strong and occasionally pugnacious characters are assigned to work that brings them into frequent contact. You observe them almost squaring up to one another, using strong terms on a couple of occasions. Talking informally to each one you find that neither expresses to you any personal animosity towards the other but the occasional flare-ups continue, though apparently not to the detriment of work performance.

Of course there will always be grey areas and in most cases of conflict you will want to find out more facts before you do anything else.

(i)   You would probably not intervene. There is no evidence that work is being disrupted - in fact the working day is over. It may well be that the two people happen to care very much about their work and simply have differing views on how best to do things.

(ii)   You should certainly intervene. Do not be tempted to tell those people to sort things out for themselves. If both have independently come to you with their story then there is almost certainly an issue to be mediated upon. Find out more facts and get involved.

(iii)   You should intervene. People who need to communicate in an atmosphere of trust are ceasing to talk to each other.

(iv)   Here you should probably not intervene unless the flare-ups are upsetting other people. Clearly this mode of communication is one which both parties are used to and can handle. Nothing is hidden or nasty. Everything is in the open. So long as work or the morale of colleagues do not suffer, stay out of it and monitor the situation.

A healthy and productive department will consist of people who fulfil different, complementary roles and who have very different ways of expressing themselves - the chairperson figure, the team worker, the quiet 'summariser', the motivator, the 'conscience' of the group and so on. Be aware of these roles and how changing circumstances and a general state of flux or insecurity can upset and alter them. Take care that each member of the department is allowed to express their opinion without inhibition or bullying but not, of course, to the exclusion of others.

Again, be aware of **group norms**, the unwritten rules that keep groups together, define their boundaries and assign roles to each member.

Wherever you can, work with, not against those rules - do not impose an arbitrary code of behaviour where clearly one is already at work that commands the respect and compliance of the people concerned.

3.2   PREVENTION BETTER THAN CURE

The most effective way of handling conflict is to prevent it from arising wherever possible, that is, to set out the rules of engagement and apply them in such a way that any expression of difference does not develop into negative conflict. What can you do when you suspect that the transformation is about to happen?

Do Not let Anyone Lose

If you can call a 'draw' or even better, find a way in which both sides can win you will prevent the ill effects of both losing (humiliation, low morale, loss of face, resentment, revenge) and winning at someone else's expense (arrogance, over-confidence and the desire to do it again).

We all have egos, some larger than others, and we all care to some extent what others think about us. Letting someone 'save face' when they are in a tight corner will be beneficial to both sides of an argument and even more so to those who have to work with them.

Let Both Sides Win if Possible

This is not always possible of course, but you should always see if a 'Win/Win' solution is practical. Calling a draw is, in effect, ending a quarrel over 'who gets the cake' by cutting it in two. This solution is one where you **either** find out that one of the parties would in fact prefer a different sort of 'cake' - and you just happen to know where one is - **or** where you convince both parties to stop arguing, get down to some serious 'baking' and make a 'cake' that will satisfy both their appetites. This is obviously better than calling a draw, so always ensure that you examine carefully the possibilities of creating a Win/Win situation first.

Avoid Both Sides Losing

Do not fall into the trap (a very common fault in times of stress) of creating a 'Lose/Lose' situation. This, in effect, says, 'If you cannot agree on who should have the cake then **neither** of you will have it'.

To summarise these options then

Take the cake away	= Lose/Lose
Allocate the cake to one or another **or** cut it unequally	= Win/Lose
Cut the cake down the middle	= Draw
Make a bigger cake or find a preferable alternative	= Win/Win

---

ACTION POINT 3

Which of the four ways of preventing a difference turning into a conflict are evident in the following examples? Write your answers down and state your reasons for each.

1   Two departments' light-hearted criticism of each other develops into something more serious. Their respective managers decide that a presentation of what each department does might help to ease relations and lead to better co-operation.

2   Two colleagues have strongly differing views on how the department should respond to an enquiry, by the Manager, about their preferred work patterns. The HOD tends to agree with one rather than the other and lets it be known that she will not be forwarding the other's views.

3   In the same situation, the HOD says she will give equal weight to both arguments when she passes on the department's recommendations.

4   In the same situation, the HOD tells both people that, since the department is divided, she will offer no preferences to the Manager on this issue.

Remember

Never, in the heat of the moment, create a Lose/Lose situation.

Avoid a Win/Lose wherever you can.

Accept nothing less than a Draw.

Aim at a Win/Win situation.

Remember to use these situations as **opportunities** to re-emphasise group objectives and to make progress rather than be satisfied with just returning to the status quo.

If you create a situation in which **everyone** is going to advance, then the starting point of each person or group will become increasingly irrelevant.

ACTION POINT 4

Try to recall a situation in which you resolved a potential conflict by, in effect, returning to the status quo which existed before the conflict started. Explain briefly what you did. Can you think of any ways, with the benefit of hindsight, in which you could have used the situation as an opportunity for progress of any kind?

Write down your comments and compare them with the suggestions which follow.

Advancement could be made by

■ ending a difference of opinion over the allocation of work spaces by carrying out or recommending a review of ergonomics in your place of work, to which both parties would be invited to contribute

■ stopping a long-running feud between two groups over conflicting short-term objectives by encouraging each side to 'put itself in the other's shoes' and to look at the pressures under which the other side has to work in order to create more understanding between the two

■ using a flare-up as an opportunity for two people to clear the air and get differences into the open that have been allowed to build up between them, with a view to a more open exchange of views in future

Set a Good Example

Your ability to defuse potential conflict, or, better still, redirect the energy it feeds on into a more positive channel, will be immeasurably enhanced if **you** do not fall into the trap of letting your differences develop into conflicts.

Set a good example by treating others as you would wish them to treat each other.

This relies on all the good staff management skills and on the principles of 'natural justice' which we examined in Chapter 1 of this book.

In particular you will find the following techniques useful in stressful circumstances.

Do not lose your temper. If ever there was a principle of management that should be learned before all others it is this one.

You need to

■ stay calmer than the situation around you

■ talk more quietly than the rowing parties

■ slow the pace down

■ let people cool off

■ think before you speak

■ not be provoked

It may help actually to **visualise** lists of dos and don'ts, the four forms of discussion and other acquired techniques in order to stay in control and simply to occupy your mind on something other than the bad-tempered situation you are faced with.

Do not assume anything - find out. Do not suppose you know each person's point of view - ask them to explain it in the most basic of terms and repeat it back to them to check your understanding. Do not classify people - be aware of their **actual** characteristics and roles in a group. Remember there are two kinds of people in the world - those who constantly divide the world into two kinds of people and those who do not. Be one of the latter kind.

Do not criticise any behaviour unless you can offer a practical suggestion for improving it.

Do not disclose the existence of differences of opinion unless you have good reason. Some people love to see others arguing. It is all ammunition to gossips and trouble-stirrers. Seek advice if you need it but do not get involved in idle comment.

Do not exaggerate - when you are seeking advice from above, give a true and honest version of the facts as you see them. There is a temptation to inflate the truth in order to justify your disturbing the peaceful routine of superiors with 'your problems'. Resist the temptation. If you honestly believe a situation could lead to harmful conflict and you need advice or the 'weight' of a superior to defuse it, **no further justification is required**.

Do not bear grudges - and do not let others do so.

In summary, be **objective not subjective.**

3.3   RESOLVING CONFLICT - THE WRONG WAY

For whatever reasons, differences of opinion, objectives and territorial claims do sometimes lead to real and destructive conflict. Good staff relations and communications will do much to keep conflicts to a minimum, but what do you do with the ones that slip through the net?

First, here are a few **strategies to be avoided**.

The trouble with real, full-blooded conflict is that, by definition, it is the end of the line. The stages of harmony, peaceful consistency, tension and explicit differences will have all passed. Reason is at an end, tempers are frayed and backs are against the wall. This is not the ideal climate for cool, rational responses - yet this is where it is required more than ever. The temptation for the quick, easy solution is great but should be resisted.

The following are some all too common ill judged responses to conflict:

Coercion: This means bullying, banging the table, 'knocking their heads together'. Different people will react in different ways to this, but in no case will conflict be resolved. It is the classic example of treating **symptoms** rather than **causes**. If it achieves anything at all it will be simply to brush the conflict under the carpet and create a false sense of harmony. It may even encourage more insidious and destructive methods of waging the conflict.

Pleading is a softer form of coercion, with only slightly less poor results. Again, this is a way of treating symptoms only. A manager will simply appeal to the antagonists' better nature to stop making life unpleasant for each other and their colleagues. They may or may not agree, but either way it simply drives the conflict 'underground'. It also demonstrates managerial weakness which will eventually backfire.

Arbitration is awarding 'the cake' to one or other of the warring parties or dividing it as **you** see fit. This is a dangerous response at any time but even more so once a conflict has become destructive. Sometimes, but rarely, there will be a right and a wrong side in an argument, but before that kind of decision is made you will need to be very sure of your facts and employ your best communication skills, **particularly when informing the loser**. Most of the time there will be right and wrong on both sides, and in those cases an arbitrary decision, based either on prejudice or on chance alone (for the sake of a quiet life) is not only fraught with danger but is also unimaginative and a waste of an opportunity to seek mutual gain.

Procrastination involves putting off dealing with conflict in the hope that it will go away. The decision **when** to get involved in differences between others is one of personal judgment in the final analysis, and no hard and fast rule can be applied. However, once conflict is real and is clearly disrupting work and souring relations, the act of delaying will simply make matters worse. The conflict may well go away but could easily come back in a more serious form.

Buying-off ends a conflict by giving in to one or both parties on some **other** matter. For example, you could 'solve' bitter rivalry between two colleagues by giving both new status-enhancing responsibilities; or 'solve' an argument over work space or priorities by spending money on unnecessary but highly-prized equipment which they have asked for at sometime or other. This is a dangerous downward spiral to get yourself on. It wins no respect and quickly degenerates into a form of blackmail with the demands increasing in size as time goes on.

ACTION POINT 5

Which of the inadvisable strategies which we have just looked at are apparent in the following cases? What do you think the consequence of adopting them might be? What might be better strategies in these situations?

1   'Believe me, I tried everything to get them to cooperate with each other. I tried to reason with them, explained how- they were making life impossible for everyone else including me. The funny thing is they both get on fine with me - it's just that they can't get on with each other. They both want to do each other's job for them - that's the problem. Really it's a job for one of them only, not two. They both want to be boss.'

'Have you mentioned this to the Line Manager?'

'What's the point? Nobody listens to me. Anyway, they should learn to accept the situation - everyone else has to give and take.'

'Did your reasoning with them work?'

'For a while. They both said they would give it a try - didn't want to get me in trouble. Then a week or so later we were back to square one. I was at the end of my tether by then and I just took them aside and told them straight - any more problems and I would have to give them both new responsibilities - and **not** ones they liked. To be quite honest, they looked a bit shocked to hear me talk like that. It isn't like me to lose my temper. Anyway it seems to have done the trick. Everything's quiet now.'

2   'I couldn't get them to put their backs into the new production schedule. They kept saying that the way the sales department were allowed to get all their own way meant that nobody knew from one day to the next what they were going to have to do. I must say I sympathise with them and I told them so. It's true - we just get used to one lot of major changes when we have this little lot thrown at us. That lot in Sales just don't know what havoc they cause around here. Anyway, I told them they were going to have to grin and bear it like me. To keep them happy, I've got approval for spending on some new equipment we've needed for a while and the re-furbishment of the department. It'll make everyone feel a bit more important. I'll see what happens next. If it doesn't get any better I think I'll have to have a word with the manager about how we can communicate with Sales better than we do. I'll wait and see.'

3.4 RESOLVING CONFLICT - SOME ADVISABLE TECHNIQUES

It is all very well being told that an argument or breakdown in co-operation has an underlying cause that needs tackling, when to do so might require a lot of thought, consultation, money and **time**. But what are you expected to do **now** to get work back on the rails without shelving or, worse, exacerbating the problem?

Your immediate, short term, strategy should be to follow the following steps.

1 Intervene

Once your monitoring of differences tells you that they are becoming threatening, either to one of the parties or to the work of your section or department, you should wait no longer than it takes to find a few quiet minutes in which to think and talk rationally. **Step in** and let the conflicting parties **know** that you have stepped in and **why**. This intervention could take a variety of forms, depending on the type of conflict. It could be as formal as letting two groups know, independently, that you are aware of some conflict between them and that you propose to seek a resolution - or it could be as informal and obvious as separating two bad-tempered people who are arguing.

Whatever the context, let them know that you are

■ aware of the situation

■ going to take some action

2 Separate

One way of keeping the peace is to keep people apart. The practicality of this, of course, very much depends on the circumstances in your area of work. However, if it is obvious that the immediate conflict will continue unless people are separated, and if it is at all practical to separate them, then do so. Be careful to separate both in an **equitable** fashion.

Wherever possible do not tell just one person to move or stop what they are doing - tell both. Remember how territorially oriented people can be. Let nobody lose face.

If the conflict is less face to face and more a matter of a war of attrition conducted at a distance, (by proxy, by paper, by telephone or whatever) make it clear that it must cease immediately and that there must be a 'truce' while a settlement is sought.

3 Listen and Hear

This is the central core of resolving conflict in the short term. In few other managerial situations will you have to be as much on your mettle as in this. Do not leave things to chance - be as flexible as the situation demands, but have a firm structure of enquiry techniques to fall back on, regardless of how many people you are dealing with.

Explain why you have intervened, what you have observed and that you want the conflicting parties to work out a solution together.

Be careful with your form of delivery. **Do not ask** if there is a problem, **tell** them

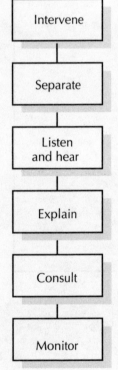

fig 3.2

there is one (Announcement) but **invite** them to join together to solve it (Problem solving). Make sure that both sides receive equal time to speak (though one or other may choose not to use their full allocation) and that both sides speak for longer than yourself. Aim for a 40/40/20 split.

Remember to make it absolutely clear when you **invite** their suggestions that it is not an invitation to be turned down lightly.

Let each person describe the **situation** as they see it. Use **theme** and **cue** techniques to set the context and invite each person's interpretation of events.

For example

(Theme) 'I have noticed a steady deterioration in relations between the two of you. It is getting to the stage where neither of you is able to concentrate fully on your work. I want whatever is the cause out in the open and sorted out before the rest of the department gets involved.

(Cue) Now, what is the problem from your point of view, Graham?'

Use **priming** and **probing** techniques to keep the facts flowing and to get more information. Sometimes both sides will be only too eager to get things off their chest but at other times you will be faced with stony **silence** or just a **continuation** of the slanging match that you have interrupted.

For example

'You want to know the problem? There's the problem sitting opposite.'

Keep calm and do not let the slanging match resume. Prime and probe for the whole story.

For example

'Well clearly you feel some antagonism towards Julia, but if we are going to sort this out you will both need to know how you see things from your own point of view. I am not looking for winners and losers. Let's hear your side of things, then Julia can tell us hers.'

Remember, it is not just you who needs to know what each person thinks - it is your job to make sure the other person knows too. Make sure they understand first before you decide whether or not to probe deeper.

Summarise at natural breaks in the conversation. Summarise at the end. Check your understanding by questioning.

Neutralise irrelevant comment or unfair tactics by identifying them and by **letting the perpetrator know** that you have identified them. Appeal to reason - do not **blame** anyone for using these tactics.

Focus the discussion back onto its original theme.

Have each person list the possible options to their respective behavioural responses - and have them assess the consequences of those reactions. The purpose of this is to encourage both parties to **stand back** from the bone of contention, look around and see if there are any other options which might address the needs of both sides.

If the mood is right, you should let this turn into a brainstorming session in which both sides throw in ideas on the explicit understanding that, at this stage, **nobody is agreeing to, or accepting anything**.

Role-reversal may help, if you feel that the mood and level of co-dividual 'step into the other person's shoes' and letting the one express the feelings of the other side as they see those feelings. Let the person whose feelings are being expressed have an opportunity to confirm or reject this version. Even go to the extent of asking one party to give what they consider to be a reasonable solution from the other person's point of view.

It is important that as you gradually edge towards a solution, you keep both parties with you so that they can be more or less equally satisfied with what is emerging. When a likely solution does emerge, have each person state the solution **as they see it**. Make sure that both people's understanding is **the same**.

Then make sure it **is agreed** - that it is accepted by both sides as a basis for future relations to which they will both agree.

It should be a plan of **action** wherever possible.

Make the agreement as formal as circumstances allow - even to the point of putting it in writing and having both parties sign:

Do all you can to maintain a businesslike atmosphere.

Let both parties know that you will be monitoring progress.

The **agreement**, the fact that it is something arrived at jointly, is as important as the solution itself.

4 Explain

Whatever the outcome of that session, it is your job to summarise the agreement or agreed next-stage and to explain what you **can** do to help. You may need to consult or gain advice from elsewhere; you may need to talk to others, perhaps witnesses or those with a legitimate interest in the outcome.

Whatever you decide you need to do next, explain and never promise anything you cannot deliver. If the two parties' agreement requires some third party action, (eg. the authorisation of new working arrangements) then only promise what you know you can achieve and do **not** throw into the melting pot any ideal but unrealistic circumstance.

For example

'We are all agreed on what you two are going to do and we all know that this will be greatly helped if I can get that authorisation I mentioned. You both know I cannot guarantee that, but I will do what I can and we will reconvene tomorrow so that I can report back and, if necessary, look again at how we can facilitate the working of our agreement.'

If the eventual, long-term solution requires time, resources or the involvement of others, then explain that you will investigate this - and give no more than a realistic estimation as to the likelihood of its being achieved.

5 Consult

Take all the advice you think you need - your colleagues may have had similar experiences.

Seek any approval you may need for the solution. **Check** your lines of communication and authority.

Keep to the facts. Do not understate or exaggerate the importance of the conflict.

6 Monitor

You should monitor how the agreement is faring - and do so visibly. Talk to the individuals concerned, but also keep a watchful eye from a distance. If it seems to be breaking down, step in quickly before any serious damage occurs.

Go through the procedures again if necessary.

3.5   THE LONGER TERM

By following the steps we have just examined, you will not simply treat the symptoms of conflict but you will identify, isolate and start treating the causes.

Your role thereafter is not just to monitor progress and stop the conflict coming to a head again, but to use this as an **opportunity** to market a sense of shared values and aims, and to make progress by positively improving the structures and lines of communication which brought about territorial claims or differences in ideologies.

In particular you should concentrate on

■ re-emphasising and, if necessary, redefining common values and goals. This is **not** simply a matter of appealing to people's better nature and asking them to sink their differences for the sake of the common good. It is an exercise as much in hard headed structural management as in abstract notions. If overlapping territories of influence or responsibility have caused conflict, then look at how respective job functions can be brought into harness so that both pull in the same direction

■ finding a 'Win/Win' solution. This is the search not for a long-term compromise but for a creative solution that **advances** both parties' interests by co-operative means

CHAPTER SUMMARY

Having completed this chapter you should now

■ understand the importance of creating a working climate that encourages the expression of differences

■ be able to put into practice the skills that will minimise the chances of those differences becoming harmful conflict

■ be aware of the dangers inherent in the more common mistaken approaches to resolving conflict

■ be able to put into practice the skills of mediating conflict professionally and with a purpose

If you are unsure of any of these areas, go back and re-read the relevant part(s) of the text.

4 THE NEGOTIATION BUSINESS

In the last chapter we looked at the handling of conflict between people or groups where you were essentially acting in a mediator's capacity. We will now be looking at those techniques you will need when you are one party negotiating with another.

As you read through this chapter you should bear the following two points in mind

- by 'negotiation' we mean 'going about your work and pursuing your interests in a way which interacts with the work and interests of others'. In other words, we will be treating the concept in the broadest terms, as defined in Chapter 1

- the techniques you will be looking at are **not** methods of winning arguments, tricking the opposition or generally getting your own way. They are designed for the pursuit of mutual gain and the furtherance of good working relations

You will need, therefore, to understand **what 'negotiation' means and in what circumstances you will practise it**. In any negotiation, issues can become clouded, so you will need to be aware of the importance of concentrating on **'interests'** rather than **'positions'**. This will necessarily involve methods of **separating the people from the problem**. To do well in any negotiation, you have to be **assertive of your interests while allowing the other party to advance their own**. This does not mean using 'tricks' to achieve one's aim, so you will also need to adopt methods of overcoming unprincipled negotiation tactics and setting the negotiation back on its course. We shall examine all of these points in this chapter.

4.1 WHAT IS NEGOTIATION?

We saw in Chapter 1 that negotiation is not just one, seemingly negative or distracting part of being in management - it actually is the **essence** of management. Without negotiation - without the dynamic effect of trading in whatever tangible or intangible commodity - there can be little advancement for either party or the organisation to which they belong.

We also noted that negotiation is all around and that people do it all the time, sometimes without even thinking, and most of the time extremely competently.

And yet, when it comes to the slightly more formal setting and where the point at issue is important and the outcome unknowable, those instinctive reactions that we display as social and co-operative creatures let us down, are forgotten or are consciously suppressed.

This is yet another area where the acquisition of skills and techniques will substantially make up for our unreliable instincts.

But first let us look at what negotiation means to you.

Negotiation occurs every time

■ the interests of one person or group are dependent on the actions or resources of another person or group who also have interests to pursue **and**

■ those respective interests are pursued by co-operative means

In Chapter 1 we looked at some diverse examples of negotiating from the important right down to the comparatively trivial. Every one of those examples contained the interdependence of interests and the co-operative means of advancing them.

ACTION POINT 1

Think of 6 examples of negotiating in your sphere of work - both the obvious and the less obvious types. Write your examples down indicating the subject of the negotiation and the type of person or group you negotiate with. Compare your answers with what follows.

Examples of negotiation in the work context could include

- buying goods or services from a supplier

- agreeing the boundaries of contingent work areas

- putting your case that extra resources be given to your departmental staff

- assigning unpopular work

- coming to terms with a Head of Department or your own line-manager with differing views or priorities

- agreeing on specific elements of working conditions where you and your group have conflicting views

- responding to discipline problems where the other person or group has a legitimate case which they have pursued by unacceptable means

All of these are negotiations because each side has a legitimate interest to pursue and will need to co-operate to some extent with the other side in order both to pursue those interests and to maintain the businesslike atmosphere essential to future negotiations.

You may also have identified one or more examples of negotiation which you find difficult and try to put off or avoid. It is those latter examples we will concentrate on in this chapter.

First let us look at why negotiating can be such a problem or a chore.

4.2   THE PROBLEM WITH NEGOTIATING...

You may be the kind of person who enjoys negotiating. Even if you are, you should be aware of why others might dislike it and check your confidence in your ability to negotiate with the points made in the rest of this chapter.

The main problems associated with negotiation are included in the following typical comments:

'It takes up far too much of my time'

'I find it hard to keep my cool'

'I always seem to come out second best'

'No matter how hard I stick to my guns, I end up giving in'

'They are just out for what they can get - it's my job to give them as little as I can get away with. It's the law of the jungle really'

'I'm never sure my boss will back me up'

'Just when you think you're there, they go and change their minds'

'They know I'm just trying to get as much as I can, and you can tell they hate me for it'

'Just when I have got the hang of the game - they go and move the goal posts'

and so on.

ACTION POINT 2

How would you express your attitude to negotiating?

If you enjoy it say why, if not, why not.

What improvement in your ability would you most like to achieve?

Write your ideas below and compare your answers with what follows.

You may have said that you

■ would like to get it over with in a more businesslike way

■ want to be able to control your temper

■ want to get what you want without upsetting the other side

■ would like to be sure you are going to be backed up on your side

■ wish you could be sure that they will stick to the agreement that is eventually reached

■ would like to be able to negotiate from a position of greater strength

We will now go systematically through each principle and technique of negotiating illustrating the common pitfalls and the right approach in each context.

Throughout the rest of this chapter the word **'partner'** is used to describe the person or group you may be negotiating with - in recognition of the fact that you are both in 'business' together.

4.3   DO NOT NEGOTIATE THE UNNEGOTIABLE

Having seen how much of work consists of negotiation, it is important to be aware that there are some issues and contexts where negotiation is inappropriate and will only complicate or hinder relations.

In those circumstances it is best simply to make the situation absolutely clear and not to suggest there is room for manoeuvre or compromise.

Such occasions could be

1   Breaches of important company procedures

2   Personal working preferences that cut across race, sex or other discrimination legislation

3   Management decisions that are to be implemented without debate

4   Agreements already arrived at by your managerial colleagues

5   Situations where bilateral agreements do not take adequate consideration of the legitimate interests of third parties

Let's look at each one in more detail.

1   Where important company procedures are involved and formal disciplinary, bargaining or other procedures are clearly laid down, you should never attempt to solve the problem informally or alone. Do not

give the impression that you are open to compromise.

2   If a member of your staff wishes to come to some arrangement with you about working procedures or relationships and that person's preferences are based on grounds of sex, race or religion, you must not entertain the suggestion. To do so would be wrong and could be unlawful.

3&4   You should not use negotiating or problem-solving terminology or inferences when the message you have been charged to pass on is really an announcement. Do not apologise when passing on unpalatable facts or decisions. Be clear and firm.

5   Be aware of the interests of third parties. Do not start discussions until you are sure that you are not compromising or ignoring other people's or department's concerns.

ACTION POINT 3

Think of an example of each of the above contexts where **negotiation is inappropriate**. Describe how someone might fall into these traps in your sphere of work.

Write your ideas down.

4.4 BE AHEAD OF THE GAME

You have now established that entering this particular negotiation would not

- prejudice company policy
- be unlawful
- compromise existing agreements
- undermine a non-negotiable state of affairs
- undercut your colleagues' positions
- ignore other interests

What you must now do is start and, if possible, complete your negotiating **before you become committed to any policy** that could undermine your position. This is not a trick - it is just efficient business practice and will, if anything, win the respect of your negotiating partner.

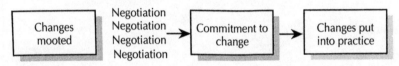

fig 4.1

Consider this example: Your department is about to introduce a new delivery approach. Once it is in place, it cannot be set aside without great disruption. In order to implement the new approach, you need to agree some changes to the work patterns of your staff. You have established that these new practices can be negotiated informally without the formal collective bargaining machinery coming into play. You have two options - you can have those new practices discussed and agreed quickly before the 'go button' is pressed, or you can wait until everything cranks into motion. The better strategy is clear. You should act **early** because

- you have nothing to gain by procrastinating
- you can deal more coherently in the comparative calm that precedes the introduction of major innovations
- time is on your side. Your staff are not yet seeking to gain advantage and being unreasonable in their demands by being aware that you are under pressure

Unfortunately, in the real world, it is often simply not in your power to decide when the 'go button' is pressed. Indeed, it may have already been pressed before you are made aware of the implications it has for your team.

This is where **planning** and **communicating** must be equal to the task.

If you constantly find you are having to negotiate when your partner knows that you are committed to a course of action and that you have no room in which to negotiate, (ie. agreement has to be reached) your position is untenable and you should make that fact known through the appropriate channels.

ACTION POINT 4

Try to recall an occasion where you were expected to negotiate in a situation when the other side knew that you were **'locked into'** a course of action that needed their co-operation.

What was the outcome?

How might the outcome have been different if you had been 'ahead of the game'?

The essential advantage of negotiating ahead of events rather than after is that you have an acceptable alternative to reaching agreement. Fisher and Urg in their book 'Getting to Yes' use the term **'Best Alternative to a Negotiated Agreement'** or 'BATNA'. You will meet this concept again later in this chapter. For now you should simply be aware that if you have no real alternative but to come to an agreement, and your partner knows this fact, your negotiation is compromised before it starts.

4.5 DO NOT NEGOTIATE OVER POSITIONS

The classic pattern of negotiating is for each side to make introductory bids or offers that are way out of the reach of the other party and then to 'dig in'. Each side will try to get the other side to move in their direction and will only move forwards themselves **either** if it is 'in return' for a compromise on the other side, **or** because they fear that if they did not, the other side would call off the negotiation. Both sides have an idea of where they would be happy to strike a deal but are sure the other side is trying to trick them. Neither wishes to lose face. Both are out for what they can get.

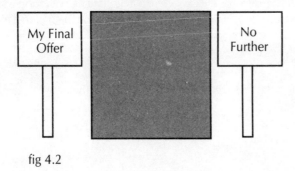

fig 4.2

The result is a great deal of expended energy, a lot of suffering and an agreement which one side will probably think they have 'won' and the other thinks they have 'lost'. Even worse, they may fail to agree, become increasingly frustrated and resentful, and retreat to their original positions watching each other suspiciously.

It is hardly surprising that negotiating is so unpopular.

Fisher and Urg identify the reasons for this.

The classic form of negotiating

■   is **inefficient** because it takes too long and wastes time and energy

■   is **unwise** - it generally produces agreements that at least one party (and sometimes both) dislikes and may seek to break

■   **endangers relationships -** whatever the outcome, relations will not have been advanced by the process and they may have actually suffered

ACTION POINT 5

Try to recall a recent negotiation in which you were involved. Describe briefly how you would rate it according to the three criteria above. How **efficiently** was it handled on both sides? Was agreement reached and if so how **wise** an agreement was it? Did relations improve, deteriorate or stay the same as a result?

4.6   THE SOFT OPTION?

What is the alternative? If you are not to be defensive and to suspect the motives of the other side, should you go to the other extreme and be soft, give ground and try to avoid confrontation?

Let's look at how this method matches up to the criteria in 4.5.

It is certainly **efficient** in the sense that it will be over quickly: either both sides will be accommodating and reach a quick agreement or the 'soft' side will be overwhelmed by the other. However, it is clearly most **unwise**. The worst that can happen is that you will gain an agreement that **does not look after your interests at all**. Even when, as is less likely, your partner responds in kind to your gentle approach, you could still arrive at an agreement that **suits neither side as well as it could**. There may well have been concessions that each side would readily have given up to the other if only they had asked, that is, a net gain for both sides and **an absolute** gain for the whole.

Not only is it unwise, it is also **unimaginative** and **unambitious**. The opportunity for both sides to gain at minimal cost to the other is lost.

It is, finally, potentially **disastrous for relations** between the two. The 'soft' side will either continue to neglect its interests and in fact bring 'business' to an end between the two parties, or, as is more likely, will allow itself to be pushed just so far and then turn on the advancing side in an over-aggressive and irrational manner. This option, the 'Soft Option' is the worst of all. It combines the disadvantages of the hard line 'digging in' with the added weakness of surrender.

Let us look, by way of example, at the kind of negotiation that might take place in an industrial setting, to illustrate the true meaning of, and best strategy for, negotiating.

A company buyer is given the job of negotiating the purchase of some new equipment for a test production plan. This is a very specialised field - one supplier leads the field with several others close behind. The buyer is keen to come to a quick deal to get this pilot scheme up and running. She has quite a lot of money in her budget as a whole, but a rather low upper limit for this particular item of expenditure. Spending more on this would mean starving other vital areas of investment.

The salesman from the suppliers is well aware of his product's superiority but he wants to make a good, impressive sale to make a name for himself by winning a major new client.

They start to negotiate.

The salesman offers a reasonable price which does not truly reflect his product's standing in the marketplace but one which is nevertheless **above** the buyer's budgetary figure. The buyer makes a counter-offer below the asking price and close to the limit of her resources.

They are both extremely relieved to find such an accommodating partner, agree on a price half way between the two, shake hands and go smiling happily back to their respective corners. Then they look at what they have got.

The buyer has spent more money than she wanted to and more money than she needed to. The salesman would have settled lower still in order to establish good relations with a major new client.

The seller has sold at a discount for the return of winning over a new client. Yet if he had thought more about his company's interests and the buyer's needs, he could have **tied** this introductory price to a longer term commitment by the buying company of the purchase of further equipment at the listed price if and when the test production scheme proved successful.

Both buyer and seller could have struck a better deal for themselves and for their mutual business relationship **if both had looked more to their own interests**.

The ironical point is that the outcome could well have been the same (except for the addition of more rancour and wasted time) if both negotiators had used the hard, positional approach.

They would still have been distracted from advancing their real interests not by the urge to come to a quick and easy deal, but by their preoccupation with not giving in on the question of price.

4.7 NEGOTIATION ON INTERESTS

The deficiency in each of the approaches above should now be emerging. Both tactics look to **positions** rather than **interests**; one is hard, the other soft but the focus is the same in each. The key to negotiation is in the word **'interests'**.

It was in the interests of the **buyer** to launch a successful and cost-effective new production scheme which would lead on to a far greater investment and commitment. It was in the interests of the **seller** that this pilot scheme be successful and thereby secure his company's involvement in the long term trade that would result.

Yet **neither** interest was advanced as far as it might have been and, as a result, an opportunity for mutual gain was missed.

So, the first principle of successful negotiating is:

Look to your interests and do not adopt any position unless it is truly advantageous to those interests.

4.8 COMPATIBLE INTERESTS

You may have noticed from the example of the buyer/seller negotiation that the interests of both sides were compatible for a very simple but sometimes unapparent reason:

What the **buyer** wanted most (a cheaper price than listed in order to get a small-budgeted pilot scheme going) was something that the seller could give with comparative ease.

What the **seller** wanted most (a lucrative, long term contract) would present the buyer with little problem.

The second principle of successful negotiating therefore is:

> **Give** whatever is more valuable to your partner than to you and **take in return** what is more valuable to you than your partner.

If you look at this principle carefully you will realise that it is nothing extraordinary. In fact, it is something we all do all the time. When you buy a newspaper it is because at that time you want the newspaper more than you want the money it costs to buy one. The publisher, equally, prefers your money to the newspaper. The deal satisfies both parties.

> Negotiation is doing business

Let us look at some valuable/cheap trade-offs.

They should include:

Give	In return for
A low price now	Long term commitment
A fast sale now	A discount
A commitment to review agreement at regular intervals	Quick acceptance of its principles for a trial period
More investment in equipment	A flexible attitude to working modes
More money now	A freeze on increases for a fixed period
Acceptance of another department's prior claim on a resource	Real commitment to invest in more
Acceptance of another person's preferences in the working environment	A commitment to look at ways of accommodating them without loss of others
More training	Less restrictions on job descriptions

Although there are several situations that can complicate this compatibility of interests, this principle should be at the core of **all** of your negotiating; whether the context is buying, selling, gaining co-operation, solving conflicts of interest or whatever. We shall examine those potential complications shortly.

ACTION POINT 6

Try to recall a situation in which a negotiation you were involved in followed this principle of 'valuable/cheap' compatibility. Explain the context and how each set of interests related and were satisfied.

Then continue with the text.

4.9 SEPARATE THE PEOPLE FROM THE PROBLEM

The next step in acquiring the skills for negotiating successfully is to learn how to separate your negotiating partner from the issue you are negotiating - to assess where your interests lie, observe them assertively and imaginatively without being distracted from your course by the effects of emotion and personality. You need to

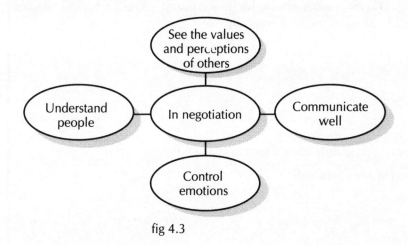

fig 4.3

1 Understand People

Nobody yet has devised a way of negotiating by computer on purely rational terms and it looks as if people are going to have to do the job for some while yet. So, you will need to understand people and their characteristics and tendencies before you can successfully separate them and their attendant complications from the business you are transacting.

Take a step back and look carefully at what **kind** of people you might have to deal with, then look at yourself and identify which **tendencies** or **emotions** might get in your way.

We all suffer to a greater or lesser extent from pressure, suspicion, misunderstanding, prejudice, failure to communicate and loss of temper. We all have our own values, priorities and styles that will not always match. Nobody will ever rid people of these characteristics, so you will have to learn how to identify them when they appear, and to control them in yourself and neutralise them in your partner.

The purpose of negotiating is twofold - to arrive at a **mutually advantageous agreement** and **to lay the foundations for future business**.

ACTION POINT 7

Which **'person problems'** are evident in the following comments?

What kind of response do you think they would provoke?

1   'You knew what the conditions were before you joined. You know I can't budge on that. Are you asking me to break company rules?'

2   A: 'I don't think you understand what I'm saying.'

    B: 'Are you saying I'm stupid?'

3   'I've told you my bosses won't let me concede any more - don't you believe me?'

4   'I've dealt with your kind before. I know what you're up to.'

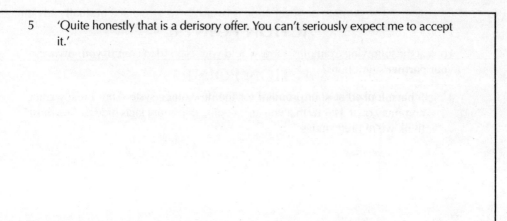

5   'Quite honestly that is a derisory offer. You can't seriously expect me to accept it.'

2 Control Emotions

Once you have recognised how you are likely to act and how your partner is likely to react (and vice versa) you should actively take steps to control those tendencies.

Everyone is different, of course, and working out what tendencies your partner has will be the first step. However, there are some rules that apply to everyone

- **do not lose your temper and do not provoke your partner to do so**. There are no winners here. Both sides benefit from the other being in control of their temper

- **do not ask or answer rhetorical questions**. Whatever you say will only make matters worse. Rhetorical questions are devices for bolstering a position, not for negotiation

- **let your partner let off steam** - whether they like to shout, name call, or whatever - if it has the side effect of allowing them to calm down, then keep quiet and let it do you a service

- **if both tempers get frayed, adjourn.** There is a saying that when you are in a hole you should stop digging. Take a time-out, cool off. Be prepared to be the one that suggests an adjournment, but do not apologise for suggesting it. Refer only to the progress of the talks you are having - keep your own behaviour or that of your partner **out** of your reasons

- **help your partner to help themself** - it is not a sign of weakness to take an insult without replying. The more controlled your partner is the better for **both** of you

ACTION POINT 8

Look at the following examples. How would you respond to control **your own** and **your partner's** emotions?

1 'I have looked at your proposal for the new office system but I really can't comment on it. I know that you are keeping important facts hidden. You must think we're pretty naive.'

2 'Why is it you always start by asking for concessions from **us**?'

3 'Surely you don't expect us to deal with these enquiries on top of our normal workload. What do you think we are - slaves?'

4 'I'm obviously getting nowhere - I might as well bang my head against a brick wall. If that's your final position we might as well stop all this endless talking and get back to doing what we get paid for.'

You may be interested in comparing your answers with the following

(i)   This is a provocative statement which needs to be handled carefully. The best way is to stay calm and state your case as honestly as you can. If you are calm, then your partner has no reason to get annoyed.

(ii)   This is a question which should not be answered. The best thing to do in this case is to allow your partner to continue.

(iii)   This is a rhetorical question which again should not be answered. By all means allow your partner to let off steam, but do not allow yourself to be drawn into making a response which will only exacerbate the situation.

(iv)   This is a good time for adjournment of negotiations. It would be as well to allow your partner some time to cool off and re-think before you restart.

3 Communicate

It is important that you **speak to be understood** and **listen to understand**.

Everything you say should have the purpose either of explaining, seeking clarification or keeping the negotiation on track and in good humour.

Do not react aggressively if it becomes clear that your partner is communicating for another purpose. Particularly when a negotiation is conducted in group form, the spokesperson will occasionally say or do something simply to impress their colleagues and to show them that their interests are being looked after. Let your partner posture and 'play to the gallery' if that is their wish. Be aware of what is happening, do not be provoked, let them do what they need to feel secure.

It is better to deal with a secure partner than an insecure one.

Do not assume that you have been understood, or even heard. In tense situations, people can be so concerned with formulating the next stage in their argument they will simply **not hear** what you say or not fully appreciate its meaning. Check that the message has got across - but do so tactfully.

'I hope I am expressing myself clearly - shall I recap?' allows your partner to listen again with the 'blame' for lack of clarity being taken by **you** rather than your partner.

'Do you understand?' on the other hand is likely to insult. Talk about **yourself** not your partner.

Listen Actively. If necessary use priming and probing cue lines. Make sure you understand and make it clear that your understanding is **not** agreement.

For example:

'Let me just be sure exactly what you're saying - correct me if I am wrong'

not

'I can't understand what you mean. Tell me again.'

Know as much about your partner as you can. Speak and act in a way that will put them at their ease. Do not do anything to annoy or upset - if your partner does not like humour in business, do not use it in your dialogue. Try to create the necessary rapport by deliberately complying with your partner's manners and style. This does not mean giving in to psychological tricks, it simply means being aware of what relaxes, annoys and motivates your partner.

Maintain a businesslike climate throughout. Keep distractions away. Keep numbers as low as possible, unless you need several 'experts' to contribute to the discussion.

Put problems first, answers second. Let your partner **work with** you to a solution even if **you** know early on in the negotiation where that solution lies.

ACTION POINT 9

You are about to enter negotiations with someone who has the characteristics listed below. What would you do to avoid or counteract these idiosyncrasies?

1 He is very busy and slightly haphazard. He likes to do the negotiating without taking time off from his normal job.

2 He is not entirely sure of his position within the department he is supposed to represent. He finds the need to show them that he is a tough negotiator.

3   He gets carried away and is prone to nervousness and hot-headedness.

4   He has quite a good sense of humour but is very touchy about references to himself.

5   He is not terribly imaginative. His first gambit is always 'What have you got to offer?' rather than 'This is what we want' - not because of any deliberate tactic but because he genuinely is unsure of what he can realistically expect out of a negotiation.

You may interested in comparing your answers with the following text.

(i) One thing you cannot afford to do is negotiate with someone who has other things on their mind. Make sure that you set a specific time to meet this person, preferably in a 'neutral' room where there are no distractions.

(ii) This person is likely to 'play to the gallery' in order to impress his colleagues. If this will make him feel more secure, allow him to do so - it may well be to your benefit ultimately.

(iii) The best way to deal with this is always to remain calm and if necessary, re-state the situation, making sure that your partner is clear on the points which you are making.

(iv) Although it may be useful to use humour when negotiating with this person, it would probably be better to avoid it so as not to annoy him by saying the wrong thing.

(v) Whenever this arises, make sure that you focus the attention on the problem, not a 'quick' solution, even if you are aware of the existence of one. You should make your partner aware of what the situation is, rather than offering him an easy way out, which may only mean that the problem will arise again at some other time.

4 Be Perceptive

Everyone has different values and beliefs. These in turn create divergences in perception and interpretation of issues and actions. What you may see as an **opportunity,** your partner may see as a **problem**. What you may see as a 'generous offer' may be genuinely viewed as an insult by your partner.

This is something you are going to have to come to terms with, so you must

- **not** blame or criticise the perceptions of your partner
- **not** assume the worst of them
- **not** put them into a situation where they risk losing face
- give your partner a 'stake' in the agreement - a reason to support it
- find out, **before** you start to negotiate, if possible, what your partner considers important and what unimportant

The fact that two people differ in their perceptions is not necessarily an obstacle to finding an agreement - in fact it can be, and often is, a positive help.

If both the customer and the newspaper publisher had preferred the price of a newspaper to the newspaper itself, then they would not have been able to do business. So it is with perceptions: whenever you trade a commodity, you do so not only in its financial currency or in the functional units in which it is normally measured, (hours, methods, relationships or whatever) but also in the emotional attachment to its principles. For example, a person who values their time more than money (at least at the rate they happen to be traded against each other) will also have a set of emotional attachments to their perception of the value of time: time wasting will upset them, social change that leads to a higher enjoyment of free time will inspire them, and so on. **Tolerating** and **accepting** these perceptions and their emotional baggage is an essential part of doing business - of understanding your partner's motives and interests.

You are **not** being asked to **like** your partner nor even to agree on perceptions or values.

It is **not** a **debate** where one side tries to convince the other of the validity of their cause or win over an attendant audience.

Negotiation is 'doing business'. If you can secure **your** priorities while allowing your partner to secure theirs - and the exchange is made at a fair rate - then you have a good agreement and the basis for more in the future.

4.10 LOOK TO YOUR INTERESTS

You have now decided that negotiation is appropriate to your needs, you are ready to avoid the emotional pitfalls and you have come to terms with the fact that differing perceptions are a plus, not a minus in negotiating.

The next hurdle you have to overcome is **to be able to identify the interests at stake in the negotiation** - not only your partner's, but your own.

Your questions should be

- What do I want out of this and in what order of priority?
- What do they want that I can give, and in what order of priority?

The subject matter of these 'interests' is almost limitless in its variety.

ACTION POINT 10

Think of what 'interests' people value in the workplace. Write down your answers.

It is your **interests**, not your **positions,** that motivate you. When trying to further your interests and improve your ability to do your job and aim at certain objectives that are consistent with your organisation's objectives, do not let any position you may take along the way get in the way of an intelligent pursuit of your interests.

That can easily happen. Look back at the earlier example of the buyer and the seller. One wanted price X, the other price Y and they settled at price Z when, all along, the price was only one of several elements that made up their real interests.

In 'Getting to Yes', Fisher and Urg illustrate this vividly in their story of two men quarrelling in a library:

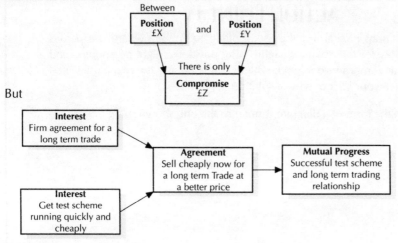

But

fig 4.4

'One wants the window open and the other wants it closed. They bicker back and forth about how much to leave it open: a crack, halfway, three quarters of the way. No solution satisfies them both. Enter the Librarian. She asks one why he wants the window open: 'To get some fresh air'. She asks the other why he wants it closed: 'To avoid the draught'. After thinking a minute, she opens wide a window in the next room, bringing in fresh air without a draught.'

Let us look at that in the form of a diagram

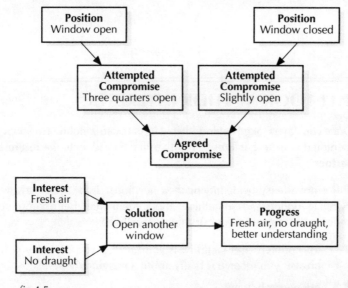

fig 4.5

ACTION POINT 11

Imagine negotiations concerning the use of office equipment where two parties both want priority for their work. Imagine what positions might be adopted and what attempts at compromise might be made. Then identify the two parties' real interests and give your idea of what a solution might be.

Illustrate this in the form of a diagram, similar to the one shown in fig 4.5.

4.11 LOOK AT THEIR INTERESTS

Once you have looked **behind** any position you feel inclined to adopt, and have identified your true interests, you then have to identify the **interests of your partner**.

This is not as easy as identifying their positions - in fact you may find yourself trying to understand something about them that they themselves do not understand. However, your first tactic should be

■ **ask**, politely and tactfully. If you find, as you probably will, that the answer you receive is really about a position then

■ **ask yourself 'why?'**

For example

Enquiry: 'Can you tell me exactly what it is you would like to result from this? How can we help you to do your job?'

Position: 'It's simple. Christine is by far the best person for the job and I want her here.'

Probing: 'Let me just examine this from another angle. You say, and I can well understand why, that this is a very important new post which requires an excellent and experienced person.'

'That's right, and I know who I want.'

'My problem is that she is in demand from other departments, as you know. Can you tell me why it must be Christine, and nobody else. The only way I will be able to achieve what you want is if I can argue on those terms with Personnel.'

'It has to be her because she's the best and the best is what we need. Anyway, if other departments can't have her that's their hard luck. We always get second best - well not this time. This time it's our turn.'

'I can understand you saying that and I appreciate how much priority you're giving to this new area of work but the fact is I cannot guarantee I can arrange her transfer; but if you can explain to me exactly what kind of qualities and experience you require, I can guarantee that you will get the kind of person and back-up that will allow you to do the job to the standards you have set. Now what are those qualities and types of experience?'

'Well, I've heard it all now. How on earth do I write a job spec. for this? I mean, it's a question of 'knowing' when someone is right isn't it.'

'Yes, to a large extent, but come on - if you are going to persuade me then you will have to persuade Personnel and they want hard facts and reasons. Give me 5 or 6 attributes this person has to have.'

Look at Obstacles

If your partner seems to be unable to move or to respond - ask **Why Not**? Make sure you know exactly **what it is** you are asking them to do, and find out what **interests** of theirs may be in the way of their agreeing to do it.

Make it Easy for Your Partner to Agree

For example, most people have ties of loyalty to their colleagues, unwritten rules of mutual treatment and behaviour. You may be asking them to do something that breaks one of those rules. They themselves may not mention the fact or even put their finger exactly on it. If your interests can be served without asking your partner to break a trust or appear to 'let down' their colleagues, then pursue that course and look at your available options within the parameters of your overall interests.

Accept the need to help your partner save face among their colleagues and not to let down or betray the people they are representing.

Negotiators often **disagree** or at least **feel uncomfortable** with the brief they have been given. They may feel they have to uphold positions they cannot justify. In those cases, do not put your negotiating partner on the spot, do not drive them into a corner. Be quick to identify this situation and do all you can to give your partner a means of principled escape from the predicament.

Be Assertive of Your Interests

It is **your** responsibility to make sure the other side understands **what** you consider important and **how much** value you attach to it.

If **you** understate the value of your interests - either by word or manner or omission, then you should not be surprised if your partner undervalues them too.

Your aim is to 'do business' - to make an exchange at the end of which you both get **more of what you want**.

Being assertive of your interests while recognising the legitimacy of your partner's is the most successful way of arriving at a fair rate of exchange. So

- state what you want to achieve clearly, rationally and firmly. Do not apologise for what you have to do or say - and do not let the tone of your voice or your mannerisms suggest an apologetic attitude

- do not suggest, or let your words or manner suggest that there is room for compromise on issues which you know you must stick to firmly

- be polite and businesslike, friendly if the occasion suits it, and always in control of your emotions. But **never** use 'throw-away' lines or tension-reducing phrases that could in any way be interpreted as insecurity or apology. In some cases that will actually mean consciously avoiding phrases which **may** come naturally to you such as

'I'm sorry about this but...'

'I'd like to help but...'

'I really wouldn't like to accept less than...'

'I'm in a difficult position...'

When what you should be saying is

'This is what the position is...'

'I cannot agree to that, however...'

'I cannot accept anything less than...'

'You would be putting me in a difficult position if...'

Do not apologise for something that is no fault of yours and may be the doing of your partner.

Never say 'may' when you mean 'must'.

Never say 'think' when you mean 'know'.

4.12 FROM INTERESTS TO SOLUTIONS

By now you should already have done much to make this stage of the negotiation more of a joint problem-solving exercise than a series of reluctant concessions.

Your principles at this stage should be

- have an open mind
- be imaginative

This is essentially the point made in Chapter 3 that if you are to aim for a 'Win/Win' solution you will need to **stand back** from the problem and not become pre-occupied with a 'cake' that will never satisfy both parties.

By all means go into a negotiation with a firm idea of your **interests**, but retain an open mind as to the **solution**. Do not assume that a solution lies somewhere **half way** between you and your partner - it may lie somewhere **in advance** of both of you.

Do not have the attitude that 'their interests are their problem'. They are, in fact, your exchange, your currency on the deal you are about to do.

Look first for **shared interests** and then for **compatible interests** - and the best way to do this is in a climate that is created by a 'brainstorming session'.

In the great majority of negotiations, a brainstorming session, as classically understood, will be impractical or inappropriate due to the informality of the circumstances - but its principles will be completely relevant to your needs. They are to

■ create a climate in which you and your partner are able to think of as many possible, relevant ideas for a solution as you can

■ do so jointly

■ avoid 'judging' **any** idea until **all** ideas have been introduced

It is up to you to create a climate of trust and mutual problem-solving in which both you and your partner feel free to throw in ideas which otherwise you may have been too guarded, cautious or simply embarrassed to mention.

You can use any context or device you feel is appropriate to the topic, mood and level of formality that prevails - checklists, a flip-chart, diagrams or simply sitting back with a coffee, away from the formality of a desk, with a pen and paper and constant assurances that the next thing you say is 'just an idea'.

ACTION POINT 12

Think back to a recent negotiation or conflict to which you were a party. With the benefit of hindsight and the removal of the emotional dimension, try to 'brainstorm' as many ideas for a solution as you think would have been worth discussing. Do so from your viewpoint and then the viewpoint of your partner or 'the other side'. Do not just consider the obvious or predictable - try to put into words some of the ideas which might lie hidden through a too 'conservative' or cautious approach to negotiating or problem solving.

Your answers will be personal, but the value lies in enabling you to see what you can do the next time you are in such a situation.

4.13 KNOW WHAT YOU ARE TRYING TO ACHIEVE

While you should not go into a negotiation with a closed mind as to what the solution may turn out to be, you must, during your talks and brainstorming sessions, keep a very steady eye on **what** you are trying to achieve and **with whom** you are trying to achieve it **at each stage**.

To do this you will need to avoid the mistake of looking only at your own interests. Look also at your partner's and take an **inquisitive interest** in your partner's **circumstances**. Is your partner completely independent or do they represent others? If so, whom? Are they likely to be backed up by their 'boss' or team or informal group? Have you got as far as you can - does either one of you need to refer back, take advice, or think about the next stage?

It may well be that the course of your negotiation simply illustrates that neither of you has the authority to do what the other is seeking. If this is the case - and the more you adopt open techniques such as brainstorming, the sooner you will find out - then you will not have wasted your time at all; you will have performed valuable scene-setting and clarification of the issues

■   focus on what you think you can achieve

■   be sure **who** from your partner's side can deliver **what**

■   do not be afraid to 'fail to agree' if it is for a reason that will lead to an eventual solution

■   do not miss the opportunity to win over your partner to your views if it becomes apparent that it is **not they but the people they represent** who actually disagree with you

■   as you concentrate on your interests, help your partner to concentrate on theirs

You may find that your role subtly changes during a negotiation and that your partner, far from opposing you, clearly sees the inherent merits of your case and is really looking for **you** to help them provide good arguments to take back and **'sell'** to those they represent.

If that is the case do all you can to help

■   **respond** to the developing situation

■   **help** your partner to agree

■   **develop** only those solutions that you know your partner **can** accept

■   **do not** force your partner into a corner

To achieve this aim of gaining what is **possible** and ignoring what is **impossible,** give your partner as much ammunition as possible. In particular

■   give reasons that appeal to **legitimacy**

■   find ways that skirt **around** 'principles' that are obstructive

■   cite precedents if there are any

■   show your partner how little what you want actually costs their side

■   avoid threats or grim warnings of the consequences of failing to agree - instead arm your partner with **offers** and opportunities available if they agree

■   be positive

Let us look at an **example**, again taken from an industrial context, in dialogue form

'May I just try to summarise how I understand your position. Correct me if I've got it wrong. You are saying that you accept my need to get this extended hours production working and you are aware of my time scale. We both want to see the company take this important new opportunity in the marketplace. However, you are very concerned about the effect on your members' work patterns and time off. You are more concerned about the effect on their morale and their home lives than, to put it bluntly, money.

You have also got a worry that this could be the 'thin end of the wedge' and could be seen by your people as a matter of principle - namely that they should not be forced to work outside the normal working day, whether or not there is more money on offer. Am I right so far?'

'More or less. I wouldn't have expressed it that way - but yes, that's about right.'

'OK. Let's look at this carefully - I reckon we are both after the same thing here.'

'That'll make a pleasant change.'

'I need to staff a shift until 9pm. I accept that people cannot be expected to be forced to do this but I would be in trouble with my people if I broke the 'single time payment only' principle - yet I accept your standpoint that your people should get something for working unsociable hours. Now the formal agreement we have doesn't help. **I** think it says we have the right to roster at any time - **you** think it says we have the right only to roster in normal working time. You want to protect your people's control over their own lives, and they would be furious if you surrendered that. They see a principle of work time versus leisure time and want to stick to it - they would only compromise on that, if at all, for an amount of money I simply have not got.

Isn't this the way forward? I will be as formal as you like in upholding the principle of the 'standard day', but I will ask your people whether or not they want to be involved in moving their work pattern to encompass the extra hours on some kind of roster pattern. Those who do will go onto this pattern in return for a lump sum which I will put onto their **standard rate** - no overtime premiums remember - and they will be rostered a **maximum** number of times in a month, say, on a regular basis. That way we both keep our principles intact, your people do only the working shift they want and the money that changes hands is within my budget and your very reasonable expectations.'

'Hold on - I would want to look very carefully at that 'maximum' number of shifts **and** the lump sum.'

'Of course - but what do you think of it as a formula?'

'It looks quite good - I think I might be able to sell this **if** the figures are satisfactory.'

ACTION POINT 13

Look back at the above dialogue and explain the manager's approach to solving the problem.

How does he present himself to his partner - what role does he adopt? Why is his partner happy to discuss the formula further?

How might the negotiation have foundered but for the manager's approach?

In our example, the manager lets his partner know that he is aware of the needs of the workforce and can, therefore, see his partner's point of view. They are both working towards joint goals in that the personal aims of each are mutually beneficial. The manager presents himself as being willing to work towards a solution rather than just negotiating over positions. Were he to have pursued the latter course, it is highly unlikely that agreement would have been reached. In this way, however, the partner can see that he is being 'consulted' and responds accordingly.

Remember - giving your partner what they want is no sign of weakness **if** it costs you little -and allows your partner to give you what you want.

A crucial tactic to use is, therefore, to concentrate on **what** you can achieve, what you can do to help your partner give it and exactly **who** it is you are trying to persuade.

4.14 OBJECTIVE CRITERIA

Not until you have used every technique and explored every avenue should you conclude that the negotiation you are conducting does not have a Win/Win solution.

You should always try to **isolate** the issue on which one person's gain has to result in the other's loss. Do not let a deadlock prevent you from agreeing on issues where there is a way forward.

When you have done this and agreed all other issues, return to the deadlocked issue and suggest recourse to an objective criterion or set of criteria - that is, some standard of work, behaviour etc that, in its general terms, is accepted as **legitimate** and relevant by **both sides**. The criterion could be precedent, 'custom and practice', other current agreements operating elsewhere, the 'going rate' and so on.

Do not let the main discussion degenerate into an argument about criteria - if necessary, brainstorm your way to agreeing criteria and let objective imagination throw in more ideas until you can find one or more on which you both agree.

Do not suggest criteria which are in reality only arguments in your favour. This will only provoke a reaction in kind from your partner. A formula for solving a problem that is jointly arrived at has a better in-built chance of success because both parties have a stake in it.

Be prepared to yield if the criterion you have chosen delivers up a solution that appears favourable to the other side, but never yield to pressure, threats or inducements that are not justifiable by reference to principle.

ACTION POINT 14

In the context of your own work, think of as many objective criteria, precedents, customs and informal 'rules' that could legitimately and relevantly be used to settle a stalemate on the following matters

1   Standards of personal behaviour in the workplace.

2 The passing of information between your department and that of your partner.

4.15 BE PREPARED TO FAIL TO AGREE

You will recall from the beginning of this chapter that, wherever possible, you should not negotiate when your partner **knows** that you cannot accept the possibility of not coming to an agreement. However, there are bound to be occasions when agreement is not going to be reached, no matter how co-operatively you work together and no matter how much you consult, or refer up, or look to objective criteria.

Be prepared for this situation. Have what Fisher and Urg call your Best Alternative to a Negotiated Agreement (**BATNA**) worked out and ready.

Often you will go into a negotiation with the following plan in mind

'Ideally I want X, but I'll be happy to settle for Y and under no circumstances will I accept less than Z.'

This is a good rough and ready plan, but it suffers from **inflexibility**. It looks to positions rather than interests. It does not cater for situations where, for some good reason you had not previously considered, it might be worth accepting a little less than your 'bottom line'.

In every area of discussion you may enter, by using the BATNA approach you will stay flexible yet secure by **knowing** exactly what the best possible alternative is to not agreeing, **assessing** its value relative to the best offer you are likely to receive, and **comparing** the two throughout the process. In this way you will be less likely to accept what you should reject, or reject what you should accept.

Looking at the example in 4.13 the best alternative to a negotiated agreement for the manager might well be the running of an extended production plan with new recruits. For his partner's group of people it may well be continuing as now without taking the offer of improved basic rates of pay. Both sides need to value those options against the **developing set of ideas** that emerge during negotiation. If, when all is said and done, the people prefer to stay as they are to anything the manager can offer, and the manager could accept the inconvenience and cost of recruitment more easily than any deal the others would accept, then they both **should** fail to agree. Failing to agree is the right thing to do.

Whether you prefer to talk in terms of BATNA or a 'bottom line', the important point is to remain **open-minded** about solutions, but absolutely **certain** about the consequences of not finding any. You do not have to agree. If the alternative to agreeing (including the consequences for future relations between the two parties) is more attractive than the best agreement you can reach, choose the former.

If you also try to find out as accurately as possible what your partner's BATNA is, you can more easily weigh up the likelihood of having to resort to your own. In the example in 4.13, the manager's negotiating partner will probably know that the manager's BATNA is expensive and inconvenient. If he can work out **how** expensive and inconvenient, he will be in a strong position when it comes to later discussions about money and rosters.

4.16 DEALING WITH HARD CASES

The Unco-operative Partner

In the real world you are bound to come into contact with those who, for one reason or another, will prefer to stick to the positional, hard-line form of negotiating. What should you do in those cases?

How do you

- avoid slipping into positional bargaining yourself?
- get your partner to talk constructively?

Here are some suggestions

- **do not retaliate**. This is rule number one. Negotiating on interests is **no less** useful when the other side decides not to do it. Stick to reason. Ask for reasons even when you know there are none. Expose the weakness of your partner's case

- **invite** ideas and criticism. Be prepared to ask your partner to 'step into your shoes'

- **keep focusing** their attention **away** from yourself and **towards** the issues

- **whenever** an unreasonable or personal attack is made, ignore it. Keep silent. Just as the best surround for a picture is blank whiteness so the best way to highlight on unreasonable attack is blank silence. Then refocus the discussion

- **ask** questions rather than state propositions. Ask for reasons, explanations, figures, summaries, precedents, objective criteria, back-up - even if you know you will receive no answer

- **keep reiterating** your enthusiasm for a **fair** solution and **your** readiness to refer to objective criteria

- **encourage any** small sign of co-operation. Welcome it, praise it, focus on it, don't let it slip

- **summarise** what you do agree on. Isolate the points where you diverge

- **if your** BATNA is more favourable than your partner seems to think, let them know just how acceptable it is

- **if all else fails** - adjourn, take stock, let tempers cool, sleep on the problem

'Dirty Tricks'

Whatever unethical or personal method your partner may use, neither return it in kind nor submit to it. Recognise it - isolate it - mention it - question its legitimacy - suggest its counterproductive effect.

Fig 4.6 shows some of the more common unscrupulous tactics you **may** come up against.

fig 4.5

Let's have a look at ways of overcoming these unscrupulous tactics.

Stressful surroundings - created by light, noise, distractions, unequal seating arrangements etc. Agree on a 'neutral' venue. Explicitly mention the problem. Do not be too polite to protect yourself but **do not accuse**. Recognise also that your partner too could be under stress. If your office or workplace is in any way intimidating, use somewhere else. A relaxed partner is much easier to deal with.

Personal abuse - sarcasm, name calling. Silence is the first response. If it persists, mention it, describe it and ask that it should cease. The more detailed, explicit and '**matter of fact**' you are when you do this, the better.

Deception - lies, half truths, unfounded rumours. Adjourn on suspicion. Check the facts. Do not accuse anyone of deception, but make it quite plain and explicit that you are aware that untrue statements have been made, or that your partner must have been 'mistaken'. At the same time be sure of **your** facts. If you do not **know** something for sure, never make it sound as if you do.

The 'unauthorised' negotiator - just when you have played all your cards, your partner says they will have to go back to their boss or group when you were given to believe they had freedom to act. You must know exactly who you are dealing with and what level of autonomy or flexibility they enjoy. There is no 'cure' for this difficulty - only prevention.

Impossible demands - make these look as impossible and unrealistic as they are. Do not give any impression that you can take them seriously - but at all times keep cool, professional and businesslike. Give reasons, explain how far the demands are wide of the mark. Avoid exclamatory or rhetorical behaviour.

'You know I cannot come near to accepting that for the following reasons...'

is far better than

'You must be joking!' or 'Do you think I can do whatever you want me to do?'

Escalating demands - just when you are on the point of agreeing, your partner suddenly raises their demands and you have nothing left to give. The best cure for this is prevention. Make sure your partner is absolutely clear about what is being offered or requested at each stage. Make it clear when you have noticed any divergence from those clear positions. Make anything **you** offer entirely conditional on the total package being agreed. Everything you put **on** the table should be put there on the explicit understanding that it **will** be withdrawn if a package is not agreed.

'Brinkmanship' - your partner pushes you right up to the point where failure to agree would cause major problems for you. In effect, they say 'I can sit here as long as it takes to get what I want': Know your facts, know your BATNA and know your partner's. If this tactic looks like emerging then be prepared to select your BATNA **well before** the delay causes you problems. Always be **the first** to be prepared not to agree. By so doing you will either call your partner's bluff or at least minimise the damage to your own interests.

The Stressful Partner

It may be just as difficult, even more so, to deal with a stressful, insecure, rushed, nervous or reluctant negotiator as with an unscrupulous one.

Do everything you can to make them relax. Do not use stressful surroundings. Reduce the level of formality.

Prime and probe for more information. Use cue lines to encourage your partner to disclose what they are trying to achieve. Use adjournments. Give your partner confidence.

ACTION POINT 15

Imagine you have passed on your responsibility for negotiating - in whatever context - to a new, less experienced colleague. Describe the tips could you give this colleague when dealing with the following

1   A partner who is in danger of having their negotiating status withdrawn by their team if not successful.

2   Someone who always asks for 'an offer' and never suggests what they will settle for.

---

3   Someone who has been negotiating for longer than you have been alive - someone who has 'seen it all before', 'knows all the tricks' and is looking to make another 'conquest'.

4   Someone who will never move on any issue until the very last minute.

You may be interested in comparing your answers with the following

(i)   Always make sure that your partner is put at their ease using the techniques which we have examined in this unit. There is not likely to be a successful outcome to negotiation if one side is under stress to 'produce the goods'.

(ii)   Ask questions, don't state propositions. You must encourage your partner to say what they want using objective criteria by which you can both work towards a solution.

(iii) Again, always keep the discussion firmly focused on the issue at hand. Do not let yourself be sidetracked onto personal issues or any other trick which your partner may resort to.

(iv)   Always make sure in this context that your partner knows and agrees to what is being offered and requested. Do not continue until you have agreement at each stage of the negotiation.

CHAPTER SUMMARY

Having completed this chapter you should now

- be aware of the fundamental importance of negotiating as a prime management function

- be able to identify those activities in your work that are, in essence, negotiations - and to identify those activities and situations where negotiation is inappropriate

- recognise the importance of negotiating on interests rather than positions

- be prepared to use techniques that help separate people from problems

- understand how to aim for solutions that rely on the compatibility of differing interests

- remember the techniques for overcoming unprincipled and unhelpful negotiating approaches and for setting the negotiation back on course

If you are unsure about any of these areas, go back and re-read the relevant part(s) of the text.

Further Reading

Drummond H	Managing Difficult Staff
	Kogan Page 1993
Eales-White R	The Power of Persuasion
	Kogan Page 1992
Fisher R and Urg W	Getting To Yes
	Hutchinson 1981
Handy C B	Understanding Organisations
	Penguin Harmondsworth 1985
Laborde G Z	Influence With Integrity
	Signatory 1983
Peters T J and Waterman R H	In Search of Excellence
	Harper and Row 1981
Wilson G	Problem Solving and Decision Making
	Kogan Page 1993